The Ethics of Virtual Worlds

Social and Legal Challenges in the Metaverse Understanding the challenges of digital ownership and identity in virtual spaces

THOMPSON CARTER

Table of Content

TABLE OF CONTENTS

INTRODUCTION 6

The Ethics of Virtual Worlds: Social and Legal Challenges in the Metaverse 6

Chapter 1 10

The Metaverse: A New Digital Frontier 10

    Conclusion 15

Chapter 2 17

Virtual Worlds 101: Understanding the Basics 17

Chapter 3 25

The Rise of the Metaverse: From Science Fiction to Reality 25

Chapter 4 33

Digital Ownership in Virtual Worlds: What Does It Mean? 33

Chapter 5 41

Digital Identity: Creating and Managing Your Online Self 41

Chapter 6 50

Social Interactions in Virtual Worlds: The Good, the Bad, and the Ugly 50

Chapter 7 58

Building Communities: The Social Structures of Virtual Worlds 58

Chapter 8 67

The Ethics of Digital Relationships: Friendships, Love, and Beyond 67

Chapter 9 76

The Power of Virtual Influence: Social Media and Online Personalities 76

Chapter 10 86

Access and Equality: Who Gets to Participate in the Metaverse? 86

Chapter 11 97

The Legal Landscape: Understanding the Metaverse's Legal Framework 97

Chapter 12 107

Intellectual Property in the Metaverse: Protecting Your Creations 107

Chapter 13 116

Digital Theft: Hacking, Scams, and Fraud in Virtual Worlds .. 116

Chapter 14 127

Data Privacy and Security: Protecting Users in the Metaverse 127

Chapter 15 137

Contract Law and Transactions in the Metaverse 137

Chapter 16 147

The Ethics of Virtual Real Estate: Ownership vs. Exploitation 147

Chapter 17 156

Free Speech vs. Regulation: Censorship and Moderation in Virtual Worlds 156

Chapter 18 164

Corporate Power in the Metaverse: Who Controls the Virtual World? 164

Chapter 19 173

Ethical Gaming: Designing Games with Responsibility 173

Chapter 20 182

Virtual Goods and the Environmental Cost: Is the Metaverse
Sustainable? 182

Chapter 21 191

The Evolution of Digital Identity: From Avatars to Biometric
Integration 191

Chapter 22 200

NFTs and the Future of Digital Ownership 200

Chapter 23 209

AI and Automation in Virtual Worlds: Who Owns What? 209

Chapter 24 218

The Future of Privacy and Security in Virtual Worlds 218

Chapter 25 228

Case Studies in Virtual World Ethics: Lessons from the Past . 228

Chapter 26 237

The Role of Governments and Regulators in the Metaverse ... 237

Chapter 27 247

The Metaverse Beyond the Horizon: A Look at What's Next . 247

INTRODUCTION

The Ethics of Virtual Worlds: Social and Legal Challenges in the Metaverse

In the past few decades, the rise of virtual worlds and digital environments has dramatically transformed how we interact with technology, connect with others, and even understand our own identity. From the early days of simple online games and text-based simulations to today's complex and immersive metaverse, digital spaces have become a fundamental part of modern life. The metaverse, in particular, represents the convergence of physical and digital realities, where users are not just passive participants but active creators, consumers, and innovators in virtual environments. Whether in the form of **online gaming**, **virtual economies**, or **social interactions**, the metaverse is growing into a new digital frontier that offers endless possibilities—but also presents serious challenges.

This book, *The Ethics of Virtual Worlds: Social and Legal Challenges in the Metaverse*, seeks to explore the evolving landscape of digital ownership, identity, and interaction in virtual spaces. As the metaverse continues to expand and influence multiple sectors, ranging from entertainment and gaming to commerce and social media, the ethical questions surrounding its use become more urgent. How should we govern virtual spaces where people can be anything and do anything? Who owns the digital goods and assets created within these spaces? What happens when people interact in ways that blur the lines between reality and virtuality? As virtual worlds continue to proliferate, these questions are not only philosophical but deeply practical, touching on issues such as **privacy, security, intellectual property**, and **social inclusion**.

At the heart of this exploration is the recognition that virtual spaces, like the physical world, are not neutral. They are created, maintained, and governed by systems, corporations, and communities—each with its own values, priorities, and vulnerabilities. The ability to create, modify, and interact within digital spaces raises significant questions about the **rights of users, ownership of virtual goods**, and the ethical implications of new technologies. It also challenges our traditional understanding of **law, governance**, and **personal identity**.

The Metaverse as a concept has shifted from being a distant, speculative future in science fiction to a **real and tangible space** where millions of people are already spending their time, money, and creativity. It encompasses not only entertainment but also commerce, education, social interaction, and even healthcare. In these spaces, people can buy **virtual real estate**, create digital art and assets, establish businesses, and even establish relationships—transforming the digital economy and society in ways that were once unimaginable. Yet, this digital utopia also

7

brings with it ethical dilemmas that cannot be ignored. From concerns about **data privacy** and **digital surveillance** to the **exploitation** of **user-generated content** and the **monopolistic power** of tech giants, the metaverse is an environment in which regulation and governance will be constantly tested.

This book breaks down these complex ethical, social, and legal issues in a comprehensive and accessible way, offering insights into the ways virtual worlds are shaping modern life and the real-world implications of their rapid development. Across the chapters, we will explore **case studies** from well-known platforms like **Second Life**, **Fortnite**, and **Roblox**, examining both their successes and ethical failures. We will also explore key topics such as **intellectual property rights** in virtual spaces, **data privacy**, the implications of **NFTs** and **virtual economies**, and the challenge of creating **inclusive, safe, and non-exploitative virtual environments**.

As we move forward into this new age of digital interaction, it is critical to address the intersection of **technology** and **ethics** in shaping the future of the metaverse. Whether you are a **developer**, a **consumer**, a **legal expert**, or simply a curious participant in these digital spaces, the stakes of these conversations are high. By understanding the **ethical dilemmas** posed by virtual worlds and actively engaging with the questions of **governance**, **privacy**, and **inclusion**, we can ensure that the metaverse becomes a space

8

where creativity, commerce, and community can thrive **safely** and **fairly** for all users.

This book is meant to be a comprehensive resource for anyone interested in understanding the complex moral, social, and legal challenges that arise as the metaverse evolves. We will explore the history, the present, and the possible future of virtual worlds, providing both **real-world case studies** and theoretical frameworks to inform the ongoing dialogue around virtual spaces. By delving into these topics, we hope to encourage thoughtful discussion about the ethical responsibilities of developers, corporations, and users in ensuring that the metaverse remains a place of opportunity, equality, and respect for all.

As we venture into the metaverse beyond the horizon, it is vital that we do so with a sense of responsibility, **awareness**, and a strong commitment to **ethical practices**. This book aims to provide the knowledge and tools necessary to navigate that journey, offering guidance for both **beginners** looking to understand the fundamental issues and **experts** seeking deeper insights into the complex intersection of **ethics, technology**, and **law** in virtual spaces. The digital future is unfolding before us, and it is up to all of us to shape it with integrity, foresight, and responsibility.

CHAPTER 1

THE METAVERSE: A NEW DIGITAL FRONTIER

Overview of the Metaverse: What It Is and How It's Evolving

The **metaverse** is often described as the next generation of the internet—a shared, persistent virtual space where people can interact with each other, digital environments, and virtual objects in real-time. It's an interconnected universe of digital environments, ranging from virtual worlds to augmented reality (AR) experiences, and it's continuously expanding.

The metaverse isn't just a single platform or game; it's a collective term for the convergence of various virtual worlds, applications, and technologies, where people can socialize, work, learn, play, and even trade virtual assets. Major tech companies like Meta (formerly Facebook), Microsoft, and Google are all pouring billions into developing the metaverse, signaling its growing importance.

At its core, the metaverse represents the idea of a **persistent virtual space**, one that exists continuously and where users' digital experiences remain intact even after they log off. This persistence allows for greater immersion and a sense of ownership, as users can build, create, and leave their mark on these spaces, which can be visited by others.

This new digital frontier is a natural progression from the internet's earlier forms, and it's fueled by technological advancements in several areas, including gaming, blockchain, and virtual reality (VR). While the metaverse is still in its early stages, it's already attracting large investments and creating new forms of digital economies, where digital assets like NFTs (Non-Fungible Tokens) and virtual real estate hold value.

Key Concepts: Virtual Reality, Augmented Reality, and Mixed Reality

To understand the metaverse, it's crucial to grasp the foundational technologies that enable these digital spaces: **Virtual Reality (VR), Augmented Reality (AR)**, and **Mixed Reality (MR)**.

1. **Virtual Reality (VR):** VR immerses users into fully digital worlds, using devices like headsets and motion controllers. Users interact with a 3D environment and become part of a virtual experience, often leaving the real world behind entirely. In the metaverse, VR will likely be the technology that powers virtual worlds where users can fully immerse themselves—think about stepping into a

digital landscape where you can walk around, explore, and interact with other people and objects in a completely simulated space.

Example: Oculus Rift, HTC Vive, and PlayStation VR are current VR headsets designed for gaming and immersive experiences, and Meta's Horizon Worlds offers VR environments for socializing and building virtual experiences.

2. **Augmented Reality (AR):** Unlike VR, AR overlays digital information onto the physical world, enriching real-life experiences with interactive digital elements. This can range from a simple display of digital objects like directional arrows on a screen to more complex visual interactions that blend the physical and digital.

   Example: Pokémon GO, the mobile game that lets players use their smartphones to capture virtual Pokémon in real-world locations, is an example of AR in action. AR glasses like Microsoft's HoloLens offer even more immersive AR experiences in professional settings, allowing virtual objects to interact with the physical world.

3. **Mixed Reality (MR):** MR combines elements of both VR and AR, allowing users to interact with both physical and

virtual environments. Unlike AR, which only overlays digital elements, MR allows virtual objects to interact with the real world in a more realistic and dynamic manner. Users can manipulate virtual objects and have them respond to their environment in real-time.

Example: Microsoft's HoloLens provides a mixed-reality experience where users can place digital objects into the physical world and interact with them using hand gestures or voice commands. This type of technology has great potential for work, design, and entertainment in the metaverse.

In the context of the metaverse, these technologies will enable different experiences. VR could power virtual worlds and gaming, while AR and MR might enhance interactions in the real world by bringing in virtual elements. The distinction between these realities will continue to blur as they converge in more sophisticated ways, allowing users to switch seamlessly between real and virtual spaces.

The Intersection of Gaming, Social Media, and Virtual Worlds

One of the key aspects of the metaverse is the **intersection of gaming, social media, and virtual worlds**, and understanding how they overlap will shed light on its potential.

1. **Gaming:** The gaming industry has long been at the forefront of developing immersive digital experiences. Games like **Fortnite** and **Minecraft** already embody aspects of the metaverse, where users not only play games but also interact, socialize, and participate in live events. Fortnite, for instance, has hosted concerts, movie screenings, and even in-game social events, blurring the lines between a video game and a social space.

   Example: In **Fortnite**, players can attend live virtual concerts by artists like Travis Scott or Ariana Grande. These events are more than just gameplay—they're shared experiences that bring players together in a new form of social interaction.

2. **Social Media:** Social media platforms are also adapting to this new digital landscape. Facebook (Meta), for example, is planning to integrate its social media features with its vision of the metaverse, using virtual avatars and virtual spaces where people can meet, chat, and interact as they do in the physical world. Social media is shifting from text-based posts and images to interactive 3D spaces where users can feel more present and engaged.

   Example: Meta's Horizon Worlds is a social VR platform where users can interact in a virtual space using avatars.

It represents a clear move toward integrating social media experiences with virtual worlds.

3. **Virtual Worlds:** Virtual worlds, such as **Second Life**, **Roblox**, and **Decentraland**, are often seen as the building blocks of the metaverse. These platforms have long allowed users to create, explore, and socialize in digital spaces. They allow for user-generated content (UGC), where participants can build and own virtual assets, creating a dynamic economy inside the virtual world.

   Example: Decentraland and **The Sandbox** are both virtual worlds built on blockchain technology, where users can own virtual real estate, buy and sell goods, and even host virtual events. These spaces represent a glimpse into the potential future of the metaverse, where user-driven economies thrive.

Conclusion

The metaverse, as a digital frontier, represents a convergence of virtual reality, augmented reality, and mixed reality technologies. It's not just about digital play spaces or immersive games; it's about creating a fully integrated and persistent digital world that encompasses social, economic, and creative activities. As these technologies evolve, they will reshape how we interact, socialize, and express ourselves, presenting new opportunities and challenges that society must address. The intersection of gaming, social media, and virtual worlds is where the metaverse will likely find its most significant impact, creating spaces for people to meet, work, play, and build together in ways we can only begin to imagine.

In the next chapters, we will delve deeper into how this virtual world is not just transforming entertainment and social interactions but also raising significant questions about ethics, legal boundaries, and the future of digital ownership and identity.

CHAPTER 2

VIRTUAL WORLDS 101: UNDERSTANDING THE BASICS

Explanation of Virtual Spaces and Their Components

At its core, a **virtual world** is a digital environment created and experienced through computers and other connected devices, where users can interact with each other and the environment. These environments are often inhabited by avatars (digital representations of users) who can explore, socialize, and interact with objects and other avatars in real-time.

Virtual spaces are constructed using a variety of components, including:

1. **3D Environments**: Most virtual worlds are designed in three dimensions, allowing users to experience depth, distance, and spatial relationships. The world can be as simple as a small room or as complex as an entire city or country. These 3D worlds are often designed using game engines like Unity or Unreal Engine, which provide the tools necessary to create immersive environments.

2. **Avatars**: Users navigate virtual worlds through avatars, which can be customized to represent them in different ways. Some avatars are simple 3D models, while others can be highly detailed, incorporating facial expressions, clothing, and unique accessories. The avatar serves as the user's presence in the virtual world and is how they interact with both the environment and other users.

3. **User Interactions**: Virtual worlds allow for dynamic interaction. Users can walk around, talk to each other, engage in games, and manipulate virtual objects. These interactions are typically facilitated through input devices like keyboards, mice, and VR controllers, which translate the user's movements into actions within the virtual world.

4. **Objects and Assets**: Virtual worlds are filled with objects—ranging from basic environmental features like trees and buildings to virtual goods like clothing, vehicles, and accessories. Some of these objects are pre-designed by the developers, while others are created and uploaded by the users themselves. Ownership and trade of digital assets (e.g., virtual goods or land) are increasingly important aspects of virtual economies.

5. **Economies**: Many virtual worlds have economies where users can buy, sell, and trade virtual goods and services. These economies often use virtual currencies, which can either be earned within the game or purchased with real

money. Some worlds integrate blockchain technology to provide unique, tradable digital assets (like NFTs).

6. **Persistence**: One of the defining features of virtual worlds is their **persistence**—the fact that the world continues to exist and evolve even when the user is not logged in. Events occur, economies fluctuate, and the environment changes in real-time, creating a more immersive and evolving experience for users.

Platforms and Environments: MMORPGs, Social Virtual Spaces, and Beyond

Virtual worlds are generally categorized based on their purpose and structure, and they often serve different kinds of interactions, from gaming to socializing to working. Here are some common types of virtual worlds and platforms that exist today:

1. **Massively Multiplayer Online Role-Playing Games (MMORPGs)**:

   MMORPGs are one of the most popular forms of virtual worlds, combining interactive digital environments with storytelling, quests, and community-driven gameplay. These worlds are "massive" in terms of the number of players they can support, often hosting tens of thousands of users at once.

   o **Examples**:

- **World of Warcraft (WoW)**: One of the most iconic MMORPGs, where players can take on roles as warriors, wizards, and other characters, completing quests and interacting with other players in a fantasy world.
- **Final Fantasy XIV**: Another MMORPG that features a rich narrative and expansive world where players can form alliances, explore, and build characters.

o **Key Features**:

- **Character Progression**: Players level up, gain skills, and collect gear.
- **PvP and PvE Content**: Players can either cooperate (PvE) or compete (PvP) with each other.
- **Guilds and Communities**: Players often form groups for cooperative play or socializing.

2. **Social Virtual Spaces**: These platforms focus on user interaction and community-building rather than gameplay or combat. Social virtual spaces allow users to meet, chat, collaborate, and engage in creative or casual activities together.

o **Examples**:

- **Second Life**: A long-standing platform where users can create avatars, socialize, buy and sell virtual property, and engage in creative activities. It's a metaverse-like environment, focused more on life simulation and social interaction.
- **Horizon Worlds (Meta)**: Meta's virtual reality social platform allows users to interact with each other in a shared 3D space, attend events, and create new environments and games.
- **VRChat**: A platform known for its extensive user-generated content, where people meet in virtual spaces to chat, play games, and even perform live events.

o **Key Features**:

- **Socializing**: Users interact through voice and text chat in shared spaces.
- **User-Created Content**: Many platforms allow users to design their own spaces, objects, and avatars.
- **Virtual Events**: Platforms often host social gatherings, concerts, and educational events.

3. **Virtual Economies and Digital Commerce**: Some virtual worlds are driven by digital economies

where users can create, buy, and sell digital goods. The concept of **virtual property** is increasingly valuable, with users investing real money into virtual assets like clothing, real estate, or even entire businesses.

- o **Examples**:
  - **Decentraland**: A blockchain-based virtual world where users can purchase, sell, and build on digital land. Its economy is driven by cryptocurrency, and assets can be traded as NFTs.
  - **The Sandbox**: A similar platform where users can buy, sell, and create virtual assets, and land is bought and sold using blockchain technology.
- o **Key Features**:
  - **Monetization**: Users can earn virtual currencies by creating and selling content or participating in economic activities.
  - **Ownership**: Blockchain allows for verified ownership of digital assets, providing security for transactions.
  - **Marketplace**: In-game stores allow users to buy, sell, and trade virtual goods.

4. **Augmented and Mixed Reality (AR/MR) Platforms**: While virtual worlds are often entirely digital, AR and MR bring elements of the digital world into real-world

environments. These platforms combine physical and digital realities to provide unique experiences for users. For instance, a user can interact with virtual objects while still being aware of their real-world surroundings.

- o **Examples**:
  - **Pokémon GO**: An AR game that blends the real world with the virtual world of Pokémon, allowing players to catch Pokémon that appear in real-world locations.
  - **Microsoft HoloLens**: An MR device that overlays digital objects onto the physical world, allowing for interactive experiences in industries such as healthcare, design, and education.
- o **Key Features**:
  - **Physical Interaction**: Users interact with virtual objects within their physical environment.
  - **Real-Time Changes**: The virtual environment adapts to changes in the real world (e.g., location, orientation).

Conclusion

Virtual worlds are not just games; they are dynamic, interactive spaces where social, economic, and creative activities unfold. Whether it's a fully immersive MMORPG or a simple social virtual space, these worlds offer users an opportunity to experience something beyond the physical world. As technology continues to evolve, virtual environments will become more integrated into our daily lives, and the distinction between the real and the virtual will become increasingly blurred.

As we continue to explore these digital realms, understanding the foundational aspects of virtual spaces—such as their components, platforms, and environments—sets the stage for delving deeper into the social, ethical, and legal challenges that come with this new frontier.

CHAPTER 3

THE RISE OF THE METAVERSE: FROM SCIENCE FICTION TO REALITY

Historical Context: Virtual Worlds Before the Metaverse

The concept of **virtual worlds** and **digital environments** is not new. Before the term "metaverse" gained widespread recognition, various forms of virtual spaces and immersive digital experiences had already been explored and developed. These early virtual worlds laid the groundwork for the metaverse, influencing both technological advancements and cultural perceptions of what digital worlds could be.

1. **The Early Days of Virtual Worlds**: The seeds of virtual worlds can be traced back to the 1960s and 1970s when early computer scientists and engineers began experimenting with graphical environments and simulations. While the technology of the time was rudimentary, these early efforts inspired the possibility of virtual spaces where users could interact.

- o **The Birth of Computer Graphics**: In the 1960s, pioneers like Ivan Sutherland developed early computer graphics tools like **Sketchpad**—a program that allowed users to draw on a screen in real-time. This laid the foundation for graphical user interfaces (GUIs) that would later evolve into immersive virtual environments.

- o **The Development of Multi-User Environments**: By the late 1970s and early 1980s, the advent of **multi-user games** and environments came into play. One of the earliest examples was **MUD1 (Multi-User Dungeon)**, launched in 1978. MUD1 was a text-based, multiplayer, real-time role-playing game where players could explore virtual worlds and interact with other players. Though primitive, MUD1 set the stage for the development of more complex and graphically rich digital spaces.

2. **The Emergence of Graphical Virtual Worlds**: In the 1990s, as graphical technology advanced, so did the potential for creating richer, more interactive digital environments. A shift from text-based worlds to 3D worlds began to take shape, and the internet became a more accessible platform for millions of users to connect.

- o **Early MUDs and MMOs**: Games like **Meridian 59** (1996) and **EverQuest** (1999) marked the

26

beginning of **Massively Multiplayer Online Games (MMOs)**, which became the first examples of immersive digital worlds where players could log in, create characters, and explore persistent environments with other players.

o **Second Life (2003)**: Developed by **Linden Lab**, **Second Life** is one of the earliest examples of a fully user-driven virtual world that allowed users to create, buy, sell, and trade digital assets. While not a game in the traditional sense, Second Life gave rise to an entirely new economy within a virtual world, offering a glimpse into the possibilities of digital ownership and virtual identity. Second Life, though niche, became a prototype for the broader concept of the metaverse.

Key Milestones in the Evolution of Digital Environments

The idea of the **metaverse**, as coined by **Neal Stephenson** in his 1992 science fiction novel *Snow Crash*, represents a convergence of technologies that enable immersive virtual experiences. However, the transition from science fiction to reality has been a long and complex journey, with several key milestones shaping the evolution of digital environments.

1. **The Birth of Virtual Reality and 3D Environments**: The early 1990s saw significant advancements in **Virtual Reality (VR)** technology, which would eventually play a critical role in the creation of the metaverse.

   o **Virtual Reality Systems**: The development of VR headsets and input devices, such as **Sega VR** (which never fully launched) and **VPL Research's DataGlove** in the 1990s, brought the concept of VR into the real world. These early VR systems, while primitive by today's standards, helped spark interest in the potential for immersive digital environments.

   o **NASA and Research Laboratories**: Throughout the 1990s, VR technology was primarily used for scientific research and simulations, with institutions like NASA experimenting with VR environments to simulate real-world scenarios.

2. **The Emergence of the Internet and Online Communities**:

   o **The Rise of Online Games**: As the internet became widely available in the 1990s and early 2000s, **Massively Multiplayer Online Games (MMOs)** like **World of Warcraft (WoW)** (2004) brought millions of players together in persistent online worlds. These games weren't just entertainment—they created global, real-time communities that interacted, collaborated, and even traded virtual goods in a shared digital space.

- o **Online Social Platforms**: At the same time, platforms like **AOL Instant Messenger**, **MySpace**, and **Facebook** transformed how people socialized online, paving the way for a more connected world. These platforms allowed users to create profiles, interact, and share experiences, which laid the groundwork for the social aspect of the metaverse.

3. **The Rise of Virtual Economies**:
   - o **Second Life (2003)**: One of the biggest milestones in the development of virtual worlds was the launch of **Second Life**, which allowed users to **create their own worlds, trade virtual goods**, and even build businesses. Second Life's introduction of a **user-driven economy**—where virtual real estate, digital clothing, and other assets had real-world value—was one of the first examples of what would later evolve into the concept of **digital ownership** and the **virtual economy** of the metaverse.
   - o **Crypto and NFTs**: The integration of blockchain technology into digital environments was a game-changer. Platforms like **Decentraland** and **The**

Sandbox use blockchain to enable **true ownership** of virtual land and digital assets through **Non-Fungible Tokens (NFTs)**. These digital assets can be bought, sold, and traded, providing real value within virtual worlds.

4. **The Growth of Social Virtual Spaces**: In the last decade, the rise of platforms like **VRChat, Roblox**, and **Horizon Worlds** has transformed virtual spaces into more social, interactive environments, allowing users to meet, chat, and create together in 3D worlds. These platforms focus not just on gaming, but on **social interaction** and **collaborative creation**, laying the groundwork for the kind of metaverse that **Meta** and other tech giants envision.

   o **Roblox (2006)**: Initially designed as a gaming platform, **Roblox** has evolved into a virtual space where players can build entire games, socialize, and create. Roblox's ability to combine **user-generated content** with a thriving digital economy has made it a precursor to the metaverse.

   o **VRChat (2014)**: An example of how social virtual reality (VR) spaces have developed, **VRChat** allows users to interact through fully immersive avatars, attend events, and even build their own worlds.

5. **Meta's Vision of the Metaverse**:

   o **Facebook Rebrand to Meta (2021)**: A pivotal moment in the evolution of the metaverse occurred when **Facebook** rebranded itself to **Meta** in 2021. With the announcement, Meta emphasized its commitment to building the metaverse, signaling that the future of the internet would be more immersive, interconnected, and virtual than ever before.

   o **Horizon Worlds**: Meta's own social VR platform, **Horizon Worlds**, is an example of the direction the company intends to take with the metaverse. Meta's ambition is to create a **fully immersive digital ecosystem** that blends work, play, and social interaction, bridging the gap between the physical and virtual worlds.

Conclusion

From its humble beginnings in the 1960s to its modern-day manifestations in platforms like **Second Life**, **Roblox**, and **Horizon Worlds**, the metaverse has evolved from science fiction to a tangible concept with the potential to revolutionize how we interact with digital spaces. Technological advancements in VR, blockchain, and online social interactions have been key milestones, leading to the creation of digital environments that are increasingly immersive and economically viable.

As the metaverse continues to develop, it holds the promise of a future where virtual and physical worlds converge, offering entirely new opportunities for socializing, working, and playing. However, with this potential also comes a set of challenges—ethical, social, and legal—that will need to be addressed as we move toward an increasingly interconnected and virtual future.

CHAPTER 4

DIGITAL OWNERSHIP IN VIRTUAL WORLDS: WHAT DOES IT MEAN?

Ownership of Virtual Goods and Spaces: NFTs, Digital Assets, and Copyright

As virtual worlds continue to evolve and become increasingly integrated into daily life, the concept of **ownership** in these environments has become a central issue. In traditional, physical worlds, ownership is easily defined by tangible property rights and clear legal frameworks. However, in virtual worlds, ownership is far more complex, particularly when it comes to digital goods, virtual spaces, and intellectual property.

1. **Virtual   Goods**:
   Virtual goods are digital items that users can buy, sell, or trade within virtual worlds. These items could range from in-game currency, clothing for avatars, virtual real estate, or other digital assets like rare collectibles. What sets virtual goods apart from physical goods is that they exist solely within the digital environment and have no tangible

33

form in the real world. However, they hold value within the context of the virtual environment and can sometimes be exchanged for real-world money.

- o **Example**: In games like **Fortnite**, players can purchase **skins, emotes**, and other cosmetic items for their avatars. Though these items have no physical form, they hold value in the community because they enhance the player's experience and represent a form of self-expression.

- o **Value in Virtual Worlds**: The value of virtual goods is often subjective, dependent on the demand within the community. Some items may be worth very little, while others may command high prices due to their rarity or desirability. For instance, limited edition skins or exclusive in-game items can become highly sought after, creating a thriving marketplace.

2. **NFTs (Non-Fungible Tokens) and Digital Ownership**: The emergence of **NFTs** has fundamentally changed how virtual goods are owned. Unlike regular digital files that can be copied and shared endlessly, NFTs are unique, verifiable assets stored on the blockchain, offering true ownership and scarcity in a digital form.

- o **What Are NFTs?**: NFTs are a type of digital asset that represent ownership of a unique item or piece of content, whether that's a digital painting,

34

music, a video clip, or virtual real estate in a metaverse. NFTs are stored on a blockchain, which ensures their authenticity and provenance, making it impossible to replicate or counterfeit the asset.

- o **Example**: A user might purchase a virtual item in **Decentraland**, a blockchain-based virtual world, where the item is represented as an NFT. This NFT serves as proof of ownership, and the owner can resell the item in an NFT marketplace or use it within the virtual space.

- o **Digital Ownership through NFTs**: By utilizing NFTs, virtual worlds and their creators are able to give users genuine ownership over their digital goods. Users are no longer merely renting items within the game; instead, they own them in a way that allows them to transfer, sell, or trade these assets as they would physical goods.

3. **Digital   Assets   and   Copyright**: One of the key challenges in virtual worlds is the **protection of intellectual property**. In the real world, intellectual property (IP) laws govern ownership rights over creations, ideas, and inventions. In the digital world, the same issues arise, but the application of these laws can be murky due to the ease with which digital assets can be copied and shared.

35

o **Copyright Protection**: In virtual worlds, **copyright laws** can be applied to protect digital content such as artwork, code, and designs created by developers or users. For instance, if a player designs a custom avatar outfit in a game like **Roblox**, that design may be protected under copyright law. Similarly, creators of virtual environments or 3D models could claim ownership of their designs through copyright.

o **Challenges with Digital Copyright**: One challenge in virtual spaces is **enforcement** of copyright. Digital content is often easily copied or shared, and virtual worlds frequently rely on community policing or platform-based moderation to prevent intellectual property theft. However, blockchain technology, through the use of NFTs, provides a new way to track ownership and protect creators' rights.

o **Example**: In **Second Life**, users are able to create their own virtual assets, such as clothing, buildings, or vehicles, and these can be bought and sold within the game. However, if someone else were to replicate and sell these assets without permission, it could lead to intellectual property disputes. This is why platforms often incorporate rules around IP ownership, ensuring creators have control over their digital goods.

Case Studies of Virtual Real Estate

Virtual real estate is an increasingly popular and valuable asset within the metaverse. As users flock to virtual worlds to create, socialize, and transact, **virtual land** has emerged as an investment opportunity. In many digital worlds, real estate is bought and sold much like physical property, with its value fluctuating based on location, rarity, and demand.

1. **Decentraland**: Decentraland is one of the most famous examples of a **blockchain-based virtual world** where users can buy, sell, and develop virtual real estate. The virtual land in Decentraland is represented as NFTs, which ensures that each plot of land has unique ownership rights. Landowners can build structures, create art installations, or even develop commercial spaces.
   o **Example of Virtual Real Estate Investment**: In 2021, an investor purchased a virtual plot of land in Decentraland for **$2.4 million**, making headlines as one of the most expensive real estate transactions in the virtual world at the time. The investor planned to develop a virtual shopping

mall on the land and lease space to brands looking to enter the metaverse.

- o **How It Works**: In Decentraland, users use **MANA**, the platform's cryptocurrency, to purchase land. Each parcel is represented by an NFT, which is tradable on the open market. This allows for true ownership of digital land, and users can either develop or resell their property.

2. **The Sandbox**: Similar to Decentraland, **The Sandbox** is another virtual world that allows users to buy, sell, and develop virtual land. The platform focuses on user-generated content and features a digital economy based on NFTs and cryptocurrency. The Sandbox's virtual land is also tokenized as NFTs, and players can create games, experiences, and businesses within their land.

- o **Example of Virtual Real Estate Use**: In **The Sandbox**, celebrities and brands have also entered the virtual real estate market. For instance, **Snoop Dogg** purchased virtual land in The Sandbox to build a virtual mansion and a Snoop-themed experience. The land he bought became a hot commodity, with other users interested in building adjacent plots to form a digital neighborhood.

- o **Value of Virtual Land**: As with real-world real estate, the value of virtual land in The Sandbox is determined by various factors like location within the world, proximity to popular areas, and the potential for development. Some plots have sold for tens of thousands of dollars, and land in areas closer to high-traffic zones often sees higher prices.

3. **Somnium Space**: **Somnium Space** is another blockchain-powered virtual reality world that offers users the ability to buy, sell, and build on virtual land. With a focus on **VR experiences**, Somnium Space allows for fully immersive 3D environments and offers landowners the ability to build VR experiences, host events, or create interactive art pieces.

   o **Example of Community-Driven Development**: In Somnium Space, virtual land is auctioned, and owners can build whatever they wish, including stores, art galleries, or even casinos. The marketplace is powered by **ETH** (Ethereum), and land can be developed into a fully interactive VR experience.

   o **Ownership Verification**: Each plot of land in Somnium Space is tokenized as an NFT, ensuring that ownership is verified through blockchain technology. This creates a new form of digital property rights that go beyond traditional virtual environments.

Conclusion

As the metaverse continues to evolve, **digital ownership** is becoming an increasingly important concept. The rise of **NFTs** and **blockchain technology** has given users the ability to own, trade, and create in virtual spaces in ways that were previously unimaginable. Whether it's virtual goods like in-game items and avatars, or virtual real estate in platforms like **Decentraland** or **The Sandbox**, the concept of ownership is no longer confined to the physical world.

However, digital ownership also raises important legal and ethical questions, particularly when it comes to intellectual property, copyright, and the control over virtual spaces. As virtual worlds continue to grow and mature, these issues will need to be addressed to ensure that ownership rights are respected, protected, and enforced across different digital environments.

The case studies of virtual real estate highlight the potential for virtual spaces to be developed into valuable assets, providing new opportunities for investment and business in the metaverse. But, like in the physical world, understanding the complexities of ownership in digital spaces is key to navigating this new frontier.

CHAPTER 5

DIGITAL IDENTITY: CREATING AND MANAGING YOUR ONLINE SELF

How Identity is Shaped in Virtual Worlds

Digital identity in virtual worlds is a multifaceted and evolving concept. In the real world, identity is typically shaped by a combination of physical traits, social relationships, cultural background, and personal experiences. However, in virtual spaces, the concept of identity becomes much more fluid, allowing individuals to experiment with and adapt their identity in ways that would be difficult or impossible in physical environments.

1. **The Fluidity of Identity in Virtual Worlds**: Virtual worlds offer users the ability to craft, modify, and even completely change their digital identities. This malleability is one of the key features that distinguishes online personas from real-world identities. While a real-world identity is largely fixed—defined by factors like appearance, age, and gender—a virtual identity can be

41

highly customizable and adaptable, depending on the platform's rules and the user's preferences.

- o **Customization of Identity**: Users can choose to present themselves as any avatar or persona they desire. For instance, someone might choose to represent themselves as a human in one space, while opting for a non-human character (e.g., an alien, animal, or mythical creature) in another. This ability to switch between different identities allows users to express different aspects of themselves or explore entirely new facets of their personality that they might not express in the physical world.

- o **Impact of Digital Identity**: A person's digital identity can impact how they are perceived in virtual worlds. For example, in social VR spaces or multiplayer games, an avatar's appearance, name, and behaviors can influence how other users interact with them. People may be judged based on how they present themselves—whether through the choices they make about their avatar's appearance, their actions in the game, or their interactions with others.

2. **The Development of Digital Identity**: The formation of a digital identity is often a dynamic process that evolves over time, especially in persistent

virtual worlds like **Second Life** or **World of Warcraft**, where users invest time in developing their avatars and digital personas. In these worlds, users' identities can grow and change based on their experiences within the environment, the people they interact with, and the roles they take on within the world.

- o **Roles and Status**: In some virtual environments, users take on roles or jobs within the community, which can be a significant part of their digital identity. Whether it's being a powerful warrior in an MMO, a designer in **Second Life**, or a digital entrepreneur in **Decentraland**, these roles can shape how users see themselves and how they are viewed by others.

Avatars, Pseudonyms, and Anonymity

One of the most important elements of digital identity in virtual worlds is the **avatar**—the digital representation of a user within the virtual space. Avatars serve as the primary vehicle for **self-representation**, and their appearance, behaviors, and choices play a significant role in how identity is constructed online.

1. **Avatars: The Face of Your Digital Identity**: An **avatar** is a 3D representation or graphical figure that acts as the user's presence in a virtual environment. The

avatar can take many forms: it can resemble the user closely, or it can be an entirely different being, such as an animal, a robot, or even an abstract shape. The choice of avatar can be a form of self-expression or a way to explore different aspects of oneself.

- o **Self-Representation**: In virtual worlds like **World of Warcraft**, **Final Fantasy XIV**, or **Roblox**, players typically create avatars that represent their character within the game. The appearance of the avatar—such as its gender, race, attire, and accessories—can reflect the user's personal preferences, social status, or role within the game world.

- o **Escape from Reality**: For many users, the avatar serves as a way to escape or differentiate themselves from their real-world identity. A person who may feel constrained by their physical appearance in the real world might choose to create an avatar that reflects an idealized version of themselves, or even something radically different. This allows for greater freedom and flexibility in how one is perceived and interacts with others in a digital space.

2. **Pseudonyms and Digital Names**: In many virtual worlds, users are required to create

pseudonyms or usernames to identify themselves. These digital names can serve multiple functions: they may reflect aspects of the user's real identity, provide anonymity, or be entirely creative and disconnected from the real world.

o **Pseudonyms and Anonymity**: The use of pseudonyms allows individuals to navigate virtual spaces without revealing their real names, which can help to preserve privacy and security. However, this anonymity can also foster a sense of **freedom**, as individuals may feel less inhibited by societal expectations when they are not identified by their real-world identity.

o **Example**: A person in a virtual gaming environment may use a pseudonym like "DarkKnight123" rather than their real name. This allows them to distance their real-world identity from their online persona, offering privacy while enabling them to participate in virtual social interactions without fear of judgment based on their physical appearance or social background.

o **The Double-Edged Sword of Anonymity**: While pseudonyms can provide freedom and allow for creative expression, they can also lead to negative behavior. Anonymity in online spaces is often associated with negative behaviors, such as trolling, harassment, and cyberbullying, because users may feel less accountable for their actions. Therefore, while pseudonyms and anonymity allow for freedom, they also pose challenges in terms of online safety and accountability.

The Role of Self-Expression in Digital Spaces

Self-expression is one of the core aspects of digital identity. In virtual spaces, users are not confined by physical appearance or limitations. Instead, they can present themselves however they see fit, using avatars, names, and behaviors to reflect different aspects of their personality, identity, or creative vision.

1. **Creative Expression through Avatars**: Virtual worlds and platforms like **Second Life**, **Roblox**, and **VRChat** allow users to design their own avatars and environments. This level of customization allows for rich self-expression, whether through clothing choices, body modifications, or entire worlds created by users themselves.

   o **Example**: In **Roblox**, users can create unique avatars with clothing, accessories, and body parts, reflecting different styles or even personalities. Players who design their avatars may express different tastes, interests, and cultures through their digital creations.

- o **Virtual Art**: Many virtual worlds also encourage users to create and share digital art, whether through custom avatars, 3D objects, or digital fashion. Platforms like **Decentraland** or **Somnium Space** allow users to showcase and even sell virtual art, blending creativity and commerce.

2. **Exploring Identity Through Virtual Spaces**: Virtual worlds also allow individuals to experiment with new identities or roles that they might not have the opportunity to explore in real life. The virtual world becomes a space where people can be whoever they want to be, and this freedom can lead to profound personal insights or creative experimentation.

- o **Gender and Identity**: Virtual spaces provide opportunities for individuals to explore gender identity in a more fluid and open environment. In these worlds, users can experiment with different avatars and gender representations without facing the societal norms and constraints often found in the physical world.

- o **Example**: Someone questioning their gender identity might choose to create a female avatar in a virtual world, allowing them to explore how they feel about this representation in a way that feels safer and more personal than making changes in real life.

3. **Virtual Identity and Real-World Impact**: Self-expression in digital spaces often spills over into the physical world, impacting how individuals see themselves and their interactions in real life. For instance, a person who creates an avatar that represents a powerful warrior or confident entrepreneur may experience a sense of empowerment that translates into their offline life.

   o **Digital Confidence**: Many users find that experimenting with digital identity enhances their confidence. The flexibility to customize how they are seen online may encourage them to express themselves more freely, helping them gain confidence in real-world interactions.

   o **Impact of Digital Identity on Mental Health**: For some, the freedom to express themselves in virtual worlds can improve their mental health, providing an outlet for creativity, stress relief, and personal exploration. However, the pressure to conform to certain social standards or idealized avatars can also contribute to issues like body dysmorphia or online identity-related anxiety.

48

Conclusion

In virtual worlds, **digital identity** is not just about creating an avatar; it is about crafting a self-presentation that reflects personal choices, values, and creative expression. From avatars and pseudonyms to the exploration of gender and personal identity, virtual worlds offer unprecedented opportunities for self-expression. However, the complexities of anonymity and the ability to switch between multiple identities also present challenges—both in terms of online behavior and personal accountability.

As the lines between the digital and physical world continue to blur, understanding the nature of digital identity will become increasingly important. How individuals manage their online selves—whether as a form of escapism, self-exploration, or creative expression—will play a crucial role in shaping the future of virtual spaces and the way we interact with each other in the metaverse.

CHAPTER 6

SOCIAL INTERACTIONS IN VIRTUAL WORLDS: THE GOOD, THE BAD, AND THE UGLY

Positive Aspects: Collaboration, Communities, and Creativity

The metaverse, with its immersive digital spaces and interconnected environments, offers significant opportunities for **social interaction**, creativity, and collaboration. As virtual worlds evolve, they create vibrant spaces where people can connect, collaborate on projects, build communities, and engage in activities that transcend the limitations of the physical world.

1. **Collaboration in Virtual Worlds**: Virtual worlds provide a unique space for **collaborative work** and problem-solving. Whether it's in gaming, virtual workspaces, or digital art, users from around the globe can come together in real-time to create, innovate, and solve problems collectively. Collaboration within these spaces is not limited by geography, and individuals from diverse backgrounds can come together to work towards a common goal.

o **Example**: In **Roblox**, players can collaborate to create entire virtual games, with one user designing the environment, another scripting the game mechanics, and others contributing art and music. This collaborative creation process encourages teamwork and harnesses the strengths of various individuals with different skill sets.

o **Workplace Collaboration**: Platforms like **Horizon Workrooms** by Meta offer virtual meeting spaces where users, wearing VR headsets, can collaborate on projects, share ideas, and participate in brainstorming sessions as if they were physically in the same room. This has the potential to revolutionize remote work, making collaboration more interactive and engaging.

2. **Communities in Virtual Worlds**: Virtual worlds are home to diverse and often **tight-knit communities** that form around shared interests, values, or activities. These communities can be centered around gaming, creativity, education, or even shared social causes. Users build connections that can sometimes be just as deep and meaningful as those formed in the physical world.

o **Example**: In **World of Warcraft** (WoW), players form guilds to cooperate on large-scale

51

raids, discuss strategies, and support each other. The guild becomes a community in which members share not only in-game experiences but also personal moments, with many long-lasting friendships formed in these virtual spaces.

- o **Supportive Communities**: In platforms like **Second Life**, people create virtual support groups for various causes, such as mental health, LGBTQ+ advocacy, or physical disabilities. These communities can offer a sense of belonging and help individuals find emotional support from like-minded people, especially for those who may feel marginalized or isolated in the real world.

3. **Creativity in Virtual Spaces**: One of the most empowering aspects of virtual worlds is the ability to **create** and **express oneself** in innovative and often unprecedented ways. Users can build their own virtual spaces, design avatars, create digital art, or develop complex games. The metaverse becomes a canvas for creative expression, where the only limitations are the user's imagination and the tools available to them.

   - o **Example: Minecraft** is an excellent example of a virtual world where creativity knows no bounds. Players can build detailed structures, cities, and even entire landscapes, pushing the limits of what can be achieved in the game. The creativity in **Minecraft** extends beyond gameplay—entire communities have been formed around the creation of stunning art, architecture, and interactive worlds.

- o **Collaborative Creativity**: Platforms like **Decentraland** and **The Sandbox** allow users to not only create but monetize their digital creations. Artists and designers can sell their virtual art, clothing, and even land to other users, building a thriving virtual economy based on creativity.

Negative Aspects: Harassment, Toxicity, and Exclusion

While virtual worlds present many opportunities for positive social interaction, they are also not without their challenges. As with any social space, online communities can sometimes foster negative behaviors that harm the experience of users, creating environments that feel unsafe or unwelcoming.

1. **Harassment**:

   One of the most pervasive issues in virtual worlds is **harassment**, where users face verbal abuse, bullying, or unwanted attention from others. Since these interactions often occur behind the veil of anonymity, individuals may feel empowered to engage in behavior they wouldn't necessarily express in real life. Harassment can take many forms, from offensive language and sexual harassment to stalking or trolling.

- o **Example**: In platforms like **VRChat**, where users interact using avatars in a fully immersive VR space, harassment can take on physical manifestations, such as unwanted virtual touching or invasive behavior. These incidents can create a distressing experience for the victims and can severely impact their sense of safety in the virtual world.

- o **In-Game Harassment**: In many multiplayer games, players encounter verbal harassment from other users, especially when performance or competition is involved. This can range from **trash-talking** to more severe forms of bullying, creating a hostile environment for those who simply wish to enjoy the game.

2. **Toxicity**:

Toxicity refers to behavior that is harmful to the community, including verbal abuse, bullying, and intentional disruption of the experience. Toxicity in virtual worlds can manifest in different ways, from **griefing** (deliberately ruining the gameplay of others) to online **flaming** (insulting or attacking other players in a malicious manner). Such behaviors can create hostile environments that discourage participation and alienate individuals from the community.

- o **Example**: In **League of Legends** and other competitive online games, toxicity is a well-documented issue. Players may use insults, verbal attacks, or even racial slurs, creating a toxic culture that deters new players and harms the overall experience. Such behavior can lead to reports and bans, but it often persists due to the anonymity that digital environments provide.

- o **Group Toxicity**: In social spaces like **Reddit**, where communities gather around shared interests, group dynamics can sometimes breed toxic behavior. Communities may rally against individuals who express different opinions, leading to **online harassment** or **exclusion** of those who don't conform to the dominant views.

3. **Exclusion**:

Exclusion in virtual spaces refers to situations where individuals or groups are **marginalized** or **left out** based on aspects of their identity, such as race, gender, sexual orientation, or skill level. While virtual worlds can offer a sense of inclusion, they can also perpetuate real-world biases and prejudices.

o **Gender and Racial Exclusion**: Women and minority groups often face higher rates of exclusion and discrimination in virtual worlds, particularly in gaming communities. Female gamers, for instance, may face sexism or harassment simply for being female. Similarly, users of certain racial backgrounds may encounter racial slurs or stereotyping, further perpetuating **discriminatory behaviors**.

o **Example**: In **Fortnite** and other multiplayer games, women players have reported being subjected to online harassment, including unwanted sexual comments and being excluded from team play based on gender. Many report that they are often treated as less skilled or "fake" gamers simply because of their gender.

o **Skill-Based Exclusion**: Another form of exclusion is based on skill level. New or casual players in games like **World of Warcraft** or **Call of Duty** may be excluded from groups or social circles because they lack the advanced skills or experience of more seasoned players. This can discourage newcomers from continuing to play or participating in the community.

Conclusion

Social interactions in virtual worlds are a double-edged sword: while they offer a vast array of opportunities for **collaboration**, **community-building**, and **creative expression**, they also present significant challenges, including **harassment**, **toxicity**, and **exclusion**. The anonymity and freedom of expression in virtual environments allow users to experiment with different personas and ideas, but it can also give rise to harmful behavior and negative social dynamics.

The key to fostering healthy virtual communities will be finding the balance between freedom of expression and protecting users from harm. Game developers, platform creators, and the broader online community will need to work together to create environments that encourage positive behavior, inclusivity, and mutual respect while addressing the problems of toxicity and harassment. By doing so, virtual worlds can truly become spaces where individuals can not only connect but also thrive in safe, supportive, and creative environments.

CHAPTER 7

BUILDING COMMUNITIES: THE SOCIAL STRUCTURES OF VIRTUAL WORLDS

How Virtual Worlds Cultivate Subcultures and Communities

Virtual worlds are more than just digital playgrounds—they are **dynamic ecosystems** where communities and subcultures evolve organically. These digital spaces are ideal for cultivating connections between users who share common interests, values, or goals, regardless of their real-world backgrounds or locations. Just as physical communities are shaped by geography, history, and culture, virtual communities are shaped by their respective platforms, activities, and social interactions.

1. **Subcultures and Shared Interests**: Virtual worlds enable the formation of **subcultures**— distinct groups of users with shared interests, behaviors, and ways of interacting within the space. These subcultures often emerge naturally as users come together around common passions, be it a specific type of gameplay, a creative pursuit, or a particular social cause.

o **Gaming Communities**: In games like **World of Warcraft** (WoW), communities often form around specific in-game roles or activities. For example, some players focus on **PvP (Player vs. Player)** combat, while others are more interested in **PvE (Player vs. Environment)** content. These players often share a common language and set of expectations for play. Over time, these shared interests create subcultures within the larger WoW community, each with its own norms and behaviors.

o **Creative Communities**: Platforms like **Second Life** and **Roblox** enable users to form creative communities based around building, designing, and creating virtual environments and assets. In these worlds, creators form tight-knit subcultures of developers, artists, and designers who share resources, collaborate on projects, and celebrate each other's work.

o **Niche Communities**: In the broader digital landscape, virtual worlds also cultivate niche communities that focus on specific interests. Whether it's **virtual fashion**, **role-playing**, **cosplay**, or **cryptocurrency** within the metaverse, these communities often find a home in platforms like **Decentraland** or **The Sandbox**,

59

where they can build virtual spaces and host events related to their passion.

2. **Affiliation and Identity**: The sense of belonging to a community is a powerful driver in virtual worlds. Just like in the real world, people gravitate toward others who share their values, interests, or objectives. Many virtual communities are built around **affiliation**, whether that's in terms of gameplay achievements, social causes, or shared experiences.

- o **Guilds and Teams**: In many multiplayer games, players can join **guilds**, **clans**, or **teams** that represent specific groups within the game. These groups provide not only a social network but also a structured framework for completing in-game objectives. Being part of a guild often leads to strong bonds of camaraderie, and members support each other, not just in gameplay, but also in life outside the game. **Guilds** may have their own names, rules, and internal hierarchies, with experienced players taking leadership roles and mentoring new members.

- o **In-Game Events**: Virtual worlds often host **events** that encourage community participation. These events can range from tournaments and competitions in gaming environments to social events like virtual art exhibits or charity fundraisers in spaces like **VRChat** or **Decentraland**. These events reinforce community ties and create a shared sense of purpose among participants.

3. **Shared Experiences and Rituals**: Many virtual worlds foster a **ritualistic culture** where certain activities or behaviors become important to the community. These rituals could involve regular group activities, special events, or even in-game celebrations that help bind players together. Such shared experiences contribute to a sense of belonging and provide structure to virtual communities.

   o **Example**: In **Final Fantasy XIV**, players gather for in-game holidays, seasonal events, and **raids**—activities that require teamwork and coordination. The social significance of these events extends beyond the game itself, creating lasting memories and friendships that stretch into the real world.

   o **Example**: In **VRChat**, people form tight-knit communities based around shared interests, whether it's a specific VR game, a social group, or even a subculture like **virtual theater**. These communities often have regular meetups or events where people gather in a virtual space to share experiences, ideas, or creations.

The Role of Moderation and Self-Regulation in Maintaining Healthy Spaces

As virtual communities grow, maintaining a healthy, welcoming environment becomes increasingly important. **Moderation** and **self-regulation** are crucial components in ensuring that virtual worlds remain places where people feel safe, respected, and valued. Without effective governance, virtual worlds can become breeding grounds for **toxic behavior**, harassment, and exclusion.

1. **Moderation: The Role of Platform Moderators**: Moderation refers to the efforts made by platform administrators or moderators to **enforce rules**, maintain order, and protect users from harmful behaviors such as harassment, hate speech, and disruptive conduct. Moderators are responsible for overseeing user interactions, managing reports, and taking action against offenders to ensure that the community remains a safe space for all users.

   o **Example**: In **Roblox**, the platform has a dedicated moderation team that reviews user-generated content, including in-game assets, avatars, and interactions. If any content is flagged for violating community guidelines—such as inappropriate language, offensive imagery, or bullying—it is either removed or restricted.

Roblox also utilizes **AI moderation** tools that can automatically detect inappropriate content before human moderators review it.

- **Example**: In **Horizon Worlds**, Meta has implemented a system of moderation where users can report offensive behavior, and moderators can issue warnings or bans to users who break the rules. Additionally, users can set their own preferences for blocking or muting others if they feel uncomfortable with specific interactions.

2. **Self-Regulation and Community-Led Moderation**: In many virtual worlds, communities are encouraged to **self-regulate** by holding members accountable for their actions. This is often facilitated through community guidelines, peer pressure, and the formation of internal systems for reporting and addressing harmful behavior. In this system, the users themselves play an active role in maintaining the social order.

- **Peer Accountability**: In platforms like **Minecraft** and **World of Warcraft**, users often form their own rules and conduct codes within guilds or subgroups. Experienced players in these communities help regulate behavior by **mentoring new players** and establishing group norms. This self-regulation can help reduce toxic behavior because members feel a sense of responsibility to protect the integrity of their community.

- o **Example**: In **Discord** servers, communities often create their own rules about acceptable behavior. Server moderators (who are typically users of the platform) can mute, warn, or ban users who engage in toxic behavior. Many **Discord communities** also set up **bots** that automatically flag harmful content or behavior, further fostering self-regulation.

3. **Automated Moderation Tools**: With the scale of modern virtual worlds, relying solely on human moderators is not always feasible. As a result, many platforms incorporate **automated moderation tools** that use artificial intelligence (AI) to detect and flag inappropriate content in real-time. These tools can scan for offensive language, inappropriate imagery, or disruptive behavior, taking immediate action when needed.

- o **Example**: **Twitch**, a popular live streaming platform, uses automated bots to detect offensive language or harmful behaviors in the chat. If the bot flags a user's message for violating the rules, it can automatically delete the message and warn the user, or even ban them depending on the severity of the behavior.

o **Example**: **Fortnite** also uses an automated reporting system where players can report toxic behavior, and the system then analyzes the reports, cross-references them with past behavior, and takes action accordingly.

Conclusion

Building and maintaining healthy communities in virtual worlds requires a delicate balance between fostering **creativity**, **collaboration**, and **self-expression** while ensuring that toxic behavior, harassment, and exclusion are minimized. Virtual worlds have the potential to create vibrant, supportive, and inclusive environments where individuals can find belonging, pursue their passions, and build meaningful relationships. However, these communities also require ongoing **moderation** and **self-regulation** to ensure that they remain safe, welcoming, and respectful places for all users.

By combining effective platform moderation with community-led initiatives and automated tools, virtual worlds can cultivate strong, thriving communities that foster positive social interaction. As these digital environments continue to evolve, the challenge will be to maintain a balance between freedom of expression and the protection of users from harmful behaviors, ensuring that virtual worlds remain spaces where people can connect, create, and collaborate in positive and meaningful ways.

CHAPTER 8

THE ETHICS OF DIGITAL RELATIONSHIPS: FRIENDSHIPS, LOVE, AND BEYOND

The Role of Romance, Friendships, and Connections in the Metaverse

The metaverse, with its immersive digital environments, has opened new avenues for social interaction, particularly in terms of **friendships**, **romantic relationships**, and **human connections**. As users create avatars and engage in shared spaces, the nature of these connections becomes increasingly complex. Digital relationships in virtual worlds mirror many aspects of real-life relationships, yet they are shaped by the unique characteristics of online environments.

1. **Friendships in the Metaverse**: Virtual worlds foster friendships that often begin with shared activities, common interests, or collaborative projects. These digital friendships can be as meaningful as those formed in the physical world, providing emotional support, social bonding, and camaraderie.

Gaming communities, virtual art spaces, and **social VR platforms** are particularly rich environments for forming friendships.

- o **Example**: In **World of Warcraft (WoW)**, players often form guilds or teams where they can interact not only for the purpose of gameplay but also to build lasting friendships. Through regular play, players get to know each other, share experiences, and support one another in both the game and in real life.

- o **Example**: In platforms like **VRChat**, users meet new people from around the world, participate in social events, and engage in spontaneous conversations, often leading to real friendships. These friendships, despite being formed virtually, can have real emotional significance for participants.

2. **Romantic Relationships in the Metaverse**: As virtual worlds become increasingly interactive and immersive, they offer a space where **romantic relationships** can blossom. Virtual dating, whether through avatar interactions or voice communication, allows people to explore intimacy in new and innovative ways. These relationships may not necessarily replace physical-world romance, but they offer a different kind of emotional connection.

- o **Example**: In **Second Life**, users often form romantic relationships that can last for months or even years. Some users even get "married" in the game, holding virtual weddings and celebrating anniversaries, demonstrating the significant emotional investment that some individuals place in these relationships.

- o **Online Dating**: Many metaverse platforms, such as **Tinder** and **OkCupid**, have incorporated digital environments to enable online dating. Some platforms go beyond typical online dating services by integrating virtual spaces where couples can meet, go on virtual dates, or engage in activities together, adding an immersive layer to the dating experience.

3. **The Role of Social Spaces in Connection**: Social interaction in virtual spaces is not just about meeting people or gaming together—it's about creating and maintaining **connections** that often transcend the boundaries of the digital realm. Social spaces in the metaverse, such as virtual clubs, lounges, or hangout spots, act as community hubs where people form lasting connections.

   - o **Example**: Platforms like **Horizon Worlds** (Meta's virtual social space) or **AltspaceVR** provide virtual meeting places where users can host or attend social events, workshops, and discussions. These spaces are designed for socializing, offering everything from casual conversations to virtual activities that help deepen human connections.

o **Example**: **Twitch** is a popular platform where streamers often build loyal communities around their content. Viewers may become friends through shared interests, interacting in chat during live streams, and forging deep connections over time.

Impact of Virtual Relationships on Real-World Emotions and Well-being

As digital relationships continue to evolve in virtual worlds, it's important to consider their **impact** on users' **real-world emotions** and **mental health**. Although the metaverse offers new opportunities for connection and interaction, virtual relationships can have both positive and negative effects on users' overall well-being.

1. **Positive Impact on Emotional Well-being**: Virtual friendships and romantic relationships can provide substantial emotional support, especially for individuals who may feel isolated or marginalized in the

physical world. The anonymity and flexibility of virtual spaces often allow users to express themselves more freely and openly than they might be able to in face-to-face interactions. This can lead to stronger emotional connections and a greater sense of community.

- o **Example**: People who struggle with social anxiety or those in remote locations can find solace in virtual communities. For instance, someone dealing with depression might find a support group in **Second Life** or **VRChat**, where others understand their struggles, offering validation and emotional support.

- o **Supportive Virtual Communities**: Communities based around specific needs, such as **LGBTQ+ support groups** or **mental health advocacy**, have emerged in virtual worlds. These communities can provide much-needed emotional support and a sense of belonging for individuals who might not have access to similar spaces in the real world.

2. **Escapism and Emotional Dependency**: While virtual relationships can provide emotional support, they can also **serve as an escape** from real-world problems, leading to **emotional dependency**. If individuals become overly reliant on their digital relationships, it can create an imbalance where the virtual

world starts to take precedence over real-world connections and responsibilities.

- o **Example**: A user might develop an emotional attachment to someone they've met in a virtual space, leading to feelings of disappointment or emotional strain if the relationship doesn't translate well into the physical world. In some cases, people might prioritize their online connections over their offline relationships, creating friction or isolation in the real world.

- o **Example**: Some users may also feel pressured to maintain their digital persona, leading to stress and anxiety. This might be particularly true in gaming communities or platforms where performance and social validation are tied to virtual status or reputation.

3. **The Blurring of Reality and Digital Identities**: As virtual relationships become more immersive, the lines between **real-world emotions** and **digital interactions** can become increasingly blurred. Users may start to attribute real-world feelings to virtual experiences, leading to confusion or emotional distress if those relationships fall apart or fail to meet expectations.

- o **Example**: A player in **World of Warcraft** may develop a deep emotional bond with another player over time, eventually leading to romantic feelings. When the virtual relationship ends—whether due to a breakup or a change in the dynamics of the game—the emotional fallout can feel very real, leaving the user with a sense of loss and sadness.

- o **Example**: Users of social VR platforms like **VRChat** or **AltspaceVR** often form lasting friendships, but the transient nature of avatars (with some people coming and going frequently) can sometimes create emotional instability. The sudden disappearance or change in behavior of a virtual friend can lead to feelings of abandonment or betrayal, even though the relationship was virtual.

4. **Mental Health Considerations**: The impact of virtual relationships on mental health can vary from person to person. For some, digital relationships offer meaningful support and can be therapeutic. For others, especially those who struggle with **attachment issues** or **mental health challenges**, virtual relationships can exacerbate feelings of loneliness, depression, or anxiety if the connection is not healthy or balanced.

- o **Example**: Some research has shown that individuals with **social anxiety** might benefit from virtual relationships, as these relationships provide a safer space to practice socializing and interacting with others. On the flip side, for individuals already struggling with **depression** or **social isolation**, the risk of becoming emotionally dependent on digital relationships may lead to further withdrawal from real-world interactions and potentially worsen mental health.

Conclusion

Virtual relationships in the metaverse represent a new frontier for human connection, offering opportunities for friendship, romance, and collaboration in ways that were previously unimagined. These digital bonds can have a profound impact on individuals' **emotional well-being**, providing support and comfort, particularly for those who might otherwise feel isolated in the physical world. However, they also raise important ethical considerations, as users must balance their digital lives with the real world to avoid emotional dependency or unhealthy attachment.

As the metaverse continues to evolve, understanding the **ethical implications** of digital relationships will be crucial. It's important to recognize that while these connections can be meaningful, they also come with unique challenges, from the risks of escapism and emotional confusion to the complexities of managing multiple identities in digital spaces. By fostering healthy virtual environments, platforms can help users form authentic, supportive relationships that contribute positively to their mental and emotional health, both online and offline.

CHAPTER 9

THE POWER OF VIRTUAL INFLUENCE: SOCIAL MEDIA AND ONLINE PERSONALITIES

The Impact of Influencers, Brands, and Celebrity Culture Within Virtual Worlds

In the metaverse, as in the physical world, **influence** plays a significant role in shaping behaviors, trends, and even economies. The rise of **influencers**, **brands**, and **celebrity culture** within virtual worlds has transformed digital spaces into highly lucrative, impactful, and sometimes contentious areas of social interaction. The presence of digital personalities in virtual environments has created new opportunities for marketing, community building, and cultural influence, but it has also raised ethical questions about authenticity, power dynamics, and exploitation.

1. **Influencers in Virtual Worlds**: Influencers in virtual spaces are individuals or avatars who hold significant sway over their followers due to their ability to attract attention, inspire behavior, or promote products. Just as social media influencers shape opinions

in real-world platforms like Instagram or TikTok, virtual influencers operate within games, social spaces, and immersive worlds, driving trends and creating new forms of digital content.

- o **Example**: In **Twitch**, content creators have massive followings, often streaming gameplay, social interactions, or creative processes. Many streamers leverage their influence to build brand partnerships, market products, or even organize virtual events and community gatherings. Their recommendations and content can have a profound effect on the gaming culture and trends within the platform.

- o **Example**: In **VRChat**, users often develop strong followings through their avatars and interactions. Some VRChat creators become virtual celebrities, hosting in-game shows, providing tutorials, or hosting meetups, all of which contribute to their growing influence. These creators can sway community behavior, inspire creativity, and even collaborate with brands for marketing purposes.

2. **Brands in Virtual Worlds**: The metaverse presents new avenues for **brands** to engage with consumers. Whether it's through branded content, virtual storefronts, or immersive advertising,

77

companies are finding ways to integrate into virtual worlds in a way that's more interactive and engaging than traditional advertising. Brands are using virtual environments to connect with younger, digitally-native audiences in innovative ways that build long-term loyalty.

- o **Example**: **Nike** and **Adidas** have ventured into virtual spaces like **Roblox** and **Fortnite**, creating virtual clothing and accessories that players can buy for their avatars. In **Decentraland** and **The Sandbox**, brands are establishing virtual showrooms or pop-up stores, where users can interact with products, purchase limited-edition virtual items, and engage in exclusive events. The idea is to blend **e-commerce** and **entertainment** into an experience that mirrors real-world shopping but with added creativity and gamification.

- o **Example**: **Gucci** and **Balenciaga** have also launched virtual fashion collections in **Fortnite** and **Roblox**, showcasing how high-end fashion brands are using virtual worlds to introduce their products to a younger, more digitally-savvy audience. This trend allows brands to experiment with fashion in a more playful, accessible way while aligning themselves with digital culture.

3. **Celebrity Culture in Virtual Spaces**: Virtual worlds have also been pivotal in the rise of **digital celebrities**, individuals or avatars who achieve fame and recognition through their activities and presence in online spaces. These virtual personalities often attract large followings, creating a subculture of fans and admirers who emulate their behaviors and ideas. Whether they are musicians, artists, or gamers, virtual celebrities can influence their audience in much the same way traditional celebrities do.

   o **Example**: In **Fortnite**, famous musicians like **Travis Scott** and **Ariana Grande** have performed virtual concerts that attract millions of players. These virtual performances are immersive experiences that blend gaming with live entertainment, creating a new form of celebrity culture within the metaverse. For both the artist and the game developers, these events are an opportunity to engage with new audiences, promote brand partnerships, and generate revenue.

   o **Example**: **Lil Nas X**, a popular music artist, has also hosted virtual concerts in Roblox, further cementing the role of celebrities in the metaverse. The ability for fans to participate in real-time experiences with their favorite celebrities adds a layer of intimacy and engagement that traditional media cannot replicate.

Ethical Considerations of Virtual Influence

The rise of influencers, brands, and celebrities within virtual worlds has brought about important ethical considerations. As virtual environments become more commercialized and intertwined with influencer culture, questions of **authenticity**, **manipulation**, **exploitation**, and **privacy** have emerged. Understanding the ethical implications of virtual influence is crucial to ensuring that digital spaces remain safe, equitable, and transparent for all users.

1. **Authenticity and Transparency**: One of the most significant ethical concerns regarding virtual influencers and brand partnerships is the issue of **authenticity**. In the metaverse, where users often interact through avatars and pseudonyms, it can be difficult to discern the real intentions behind a piece of content. The line between genuine self-expression and paid promotion can often become blurred, leading to questions about transparency.
   - o **Example**: Influencers in virtual worlds, particularly on platforms like **Twitch**, **YouTube**, or **Instagram**, often collaborate with brands to

promote products. However, some viewers may not be fully aware that the influencer is being compensated for their promotion. Disclosures, such as using hashtags like #ad or #sponsored, are intended to maintain transparency, but enforcement is inconsistent across platforms, which can create a sense of manipulation.

- o **Concerns about Authenticity**: In virtual worlds where avatars often represent idealized versions of themselves, users may feel pressured to emulate influencers' appearances, lifestyles, or behaviors, whether or not those influencers are presenting an authentic portrayal of themselves.

2. **Manipulation and Influence**: The power that influencers hold in virtual worlds can be problematic when it leads to **manipulation** of vulnerable audiences. Younger users, who are more likely to be drawn into digital spaces, can be particularly susceptible to the persuasive power of influencers who promote products, services, or ideologies that may not be in the best interest of the audience.

- o **Example**: In games like **Fortnite** or **Roblox**, where virtual goods are a key part of the experience, influencers might encourage their followers to purchase virtual items or skins. While these purchases may seem harmless, they can quickly lead to **microtransactions** that encourage kids to spend real-world money on in-game content. This raises ethical questions about the manipulation of younger users and the role of influencers in driving these behaviors.

- o **Example**: Virtual spaces are also increasingly being used for political or social influence. Celebrities or influencers with large followings may use their platforms to push certain agendas, from political views to specific social causes. While this can be empowering, it also raises concerns about **bias**, the spread of misinformation, and the use of virtual platforms to sway public opinion.

3. **Exploitation of Vulnerable Users**: Virtual worlds and their influencers can sometimes exploit **vulnerable users**, particularly in spaces where younger audiences are present. In some cases, influencers or brands target users who may lack the experience or maturity to make informed decisions about digital purchases or the content they consume. This is particularly concerning in environments where users may not fully understand the economic implications of digital transactions or how their data is being used.

- o **Example**: In virtual spaces like **Roblox**, children can easily buy virtual items or spend money on in-game purchases without fully understanding the implications. Brands targeting younger audiences can exploit this by designing game mechanics or product placements that encourage impulse spending, raising concerns about **unethical marketing practices**.

o **Influencers and Exploitation**: Some virtual influencers may exploit their followers by offering paid "exclusive" content, access to special events, or virtual gifts. While some users might view this as a fun part of the experience, others may feel obligated to spend money to maintain a sense of belonging or to be part of an influencer's inner circle.

4. **Privacy and Data Protection**: Another critical ethical concern in the metaverse is the handling of **personal data**. Influencers and brands operating within virtual worlds often gather substantial amounts of data about users, including their behaviors, preferences, and social interactions. This data is valuable for marketing and targeting, but it raises significant questions about privacy and **data protection**.

o **Example**: In virtual spaces like **Second Life** or **Horizon Worlds**, users interact with brands, and their preferences, behaviors, and interactions may be tracked. This data can then be sold or used to target users with personalized advertising, sometimes without their full understanding or consent. Ethical concerns arise when this data is used for **commercial gain** or when users are unknowingly subjected to **data exploitation**.

o **Example**: Some virtual platforms may also require users to provide personal information, such as email addresses or credit card details, to access content or purchase virtual goods. In these cases, ensuring that user data is **secured** and **protected** from unauthorized access is paramount to maintaining trust and ethical standards.

Conclusion

The presence of influencers, brands, and celebrities in the metaverse has transformed virtual worlds into powerful hubs of influence, entertainment, and commerce. These digital personalities shape trends, drive purchasing decisions, and foster community engagement in ways that were once the domain of physical-world celebrities. However, with this power comes a host of ethical considerations—from authenticity and manipulation to the exploitation of vulnerable users and the need for robust data protection.

As virtual spaces continue to grow in importance, it's crucial for both **platform creators** and **users** to engage in ethical practices that prioritize transparency, respect for privacy, and responsible use of influence. By fostering an environment that balances the power of virtual influence with ethical considerations, the metaverse can become a space where creativity, community, and commerce coexist in a way that benefits all participants.

CHAPTER 10

ACCESS AND EQUALITY: WHO GETS TO PARTICIPATE IN THE METAVERSE?

Barriers to Entry: Economic, Technological, and Social Access

The metaverse promises a new era of digital interaction, offering expansive virtual worlds for people to explore, socialize, create, and even earn a living. However, access to these spaces is not equal for everyone. **Economic, technological, and social barriers** create disparities in who can fully participate in the metaverse. As the metaverse evolves, addressing these barriers is essential to ensure inclusivity and equal opportunities for all users, regardless of their background or resources.

1. **Economic** **Barriers**:

    One of the most significant barriers to participation in the metaverse is **economic inequality**. Virtual spaces often require monetary investment in various forms—whether through the purchase of high-end hardware, virtual goods, or in-game currencies. While some platforms are free to access, many others rely on a pay-to-play or pay-to-participate model, where users must spend real money to fully enjoy the experience.

- o **Hardware Costs**: Accessing the metaverse often requires specific hardware, such as **virtual reality (VR) headsets**, powerful computers, or gaming consoles. Devices like the **Oculus Rift**, **HTC Vive**, or **PlayStation VR** can cost hundreds of dollars, and users may also need a high-performance computer to run VR applications effectively. These costs make it difficult for lower-income individuals to participate in the metaverse, especially in developing countries where such technology may be prohibitively expensive.

- o **Example**: A high-end gaming PC that meets the demands of virtual worlds or VR environments can cost upwards of $1,500. For many, this investment may be simply out of reach, limiting participation to those with disposable income or financial resources.

- o **In-Game Purchases and Microtransactions**: Many virtual worlds, particularly games and metaverse platforms, offer **in-game purchases** where users can buy virtual items like clothing, skins, or accessories for their avatars. While these items are optional, they often enhance the user's experience and social standing within the virtual world. However, purchasing these items requires additional spending, which further excludes users who cannot afford to make these purchases.

- o **Example**: In games like **Fortnite** or **Roblox**, players can buy skins or accessories for their avatars. While the game itself may be free, accessing certain content often requires real money, leading to an unequal experience for those unable to afford such purchases.

2. **Technological Barriers**: Another significant barrier is the **technological gap** between users who have access to high-speed internet, modern hardware, and advanced software, and those who do not. To access the metaverse, users need a stable internet connection, as well as devices that can run the complex software required for virtual environments. For those without reliable internet access or advanced computing devices, participating in the metaverse can be nearly impossible.

- o **Internet Access**: In many parts of the world, especially rural or underserved regions, **internet connectivity** is slow or unreliable. Even in more developed areas, data caps, throttled speeds, or poor broadband availability can make accessing immersive virtual spaces difficult or prohibitively expensive. The high bandwidth required for VR experiences and online gaming in the metaverse demands fast and stable connections that many users simply do not have access to.

o **Example**: Users living in areas with poor broadband infrastructure, such as remote or rural regions, may struggle to participate in virtual worlds, especially those that rely on high-speed internet to deliver an immersive experience, such as **Horizon Worlds** or **Decentraland**.

o **Device Limitations**: While some virtual worlds are optimized for mobile or web-based devices, many metaverse platforms demand advanced hardware like high-end VR headsets or powerful gaming PCs. Users without access to such devices are excluded from participating in these experiences, further deepening the digital divide.

o **Example**: Users with older smartphones may find it difficult to access **AR (Augmented Reality)** or **VR (Virtual Reality)** content. Platforms like **Roblox** and **Fortnite** have mobile versions, but these versions may offer a limited experience compared to the full version available on more powerful devices, creating a disparity in user experience.

3. **Social** **Barriers**:
Beyond economic and technological limitations, **social barriers** also play a role in determining who gets to participate in the metaverse. Social access is influenced by factors like **age, gender, race, cultural background**, and **disability**. Many virtual environments are designed with certain users in mind, which can inadvertently exclude others.

- o **Age and Accessibility**: While younger audiences may find the metaverse more accessible and engaging, older individuals may find it more difficult to navigate or feel alienated from the experience. The complex user interfaces, unfamiliarity with digital environments, and lack of tailored content for older users can prevent certain demographics from fully participating.

- o **Gender and Inclusivity**: Women and marginalized groups often face **gender-based discrimination** and **harassment** in online spaces, which can deter them from participating in the metaverse. Although platforms are increasingly taking measures to combat harassment, the culture of many gaming communities still reflects long-standing gender biases that prevent some individuals from feeling welcome in digital spaces.

o **Example**: Women gamers and creators often report facing **sexist harassment** in online games and virtual environments, which can create an uncomfortable or hostile atmosphere. This discourages female participation and can lead to exclusion from certain communities.

o **Disability Access**: Individuals with disabilities may face significant barriers to accessing and participating in the metaverse if platforms are not designed to accommodate their needs. For example, virtual worlds that require VR headsets may not be accessible to users with physical disabilities that prevent them from using the required equipment. Similarly, users with visual or auditory impairments may encounter barriers if platforms do not offer suitable accessibility features like screen readers, subtitles, or customizable controls.

o **Example**: In platforms like **VRChat**, users who are hearing-impaired may struggle to engage fully if the platform does not offer robust subtitles or visual cues to accompany voice interactions. Similarly, users with limited mobility may find it difficult to navigate 3D spaces using standard VR controllers.

Efforts to Make the Metaverse Inclusive and Accessible

Despite these barriers, efforts are underway to make the metaverse more **inclusive** and **accessible** to a broader audience. By addressing issues of **economic inequality**, **technological limitations**, and **social exclusion**, developers, platforms, and communities are working toward creating virtual worlds that welcome all users, regardless of their background or circumstances.

1. **Affordable and Accessible Hardware**: Some companies and platforms are striving to reduce the cost of access to the metaverse by providing more affordable hardware options and optimizing their platforms for a wider range of devices. The goal is to ensure that users, regardless of income level, can participate in virtual environments without needing to invest in expensive hardware.

   o **Example**: **Oculus Quest 2** is a relatively affordable VR headset that allows users to access a variety of metaverse experiences. Unlike earlier VR headsets that required powerful computers, the Oculus Quest 2 is a standalone device that can run virtual experiences without additional hardware. This makes it more accessible to individuals with limited financial resources.

- Example: **Web-based virtual environments**, such as **Mozilla Hubs**, allow users to access virtual spaces through web browsers on their computers or mobile devices, bypassing the need for expensive hardware like VR headsets.

2. **Improved Internet Access and Cloud-Based Solutions**: To address the issue of **internet access**, some platforms are exploring **cloud-based solutions** that reduce the reliance on high-end computing hardware and broadband speeds. These cloud solutions allow users to access virtual worlds through less powerful devices, such as smartphones or lower-end computers, while the heavy lifting of rendering and processing is done remotely on cloud servers.

   - Example: **Nvidia's Cloud Gaming** and **Google Stadia** are cloud-based platforms that allow users to stream games and virtual experiences directly to their devices without needing high-end hardware. This reduces the technological barriers to entry and makes virtual worlds more accessible to a wider range of users.

3. **Inclusive Design and Accessibility Features**: Many developers are working to make virtual worlds more inclusive by incorporating accessibility features that cater to users with disabilities. These features might include customizable controls, voice recognition, text-to-

speech options, and adaptive user interfaces that make navigating virtual spaces easier for users with a wide range of abilities.

- o **Example**: **Horizon Worlds** (Meta) and **AltspaceVR** have introduced features like customizable avatars, adjustable font sizes, and the ability to toggle visual and auditory cues, making these spaces more accessible to people with disabilities.

- o **Example**: **Minecraft** has made strides in accessibility by allowing users to customize game settings such as control schemes, color contrast, and subtitle options. This ensures that the game is playable for people with physical disabilities and those with sensory impairments.

4. **Fostering Diverse Communities**: Efforts are also being made to ensure that the metaverse reflects the diverse nature of its global user base. Platforms are incorporating features that promote inclusivity, such as ensuring that virtual spaces do not perpetuate harmful stereotypes or exclude marginalized groups. Community guidelines and moderation are key in maintaining respectful and welcoming environments for all users.

- o **Example**: **Roblox** has implemented robust moderation systems and content filtering to ensure that their platform is safe for younger users. The company also works with community leaders to ensure that marginalized groups, including women, people of color, and LGBTQ+ individuals, are represented and welcomed within the game.

- o **Example: Decentraland** and other blockchain-based virtual worlds have taken steps to ensure that their communities are inclusive and supportive. By emphasizing decentralized governance and user-driven content creation, these platforms promote a more democratic and inclusive virtual space.

Conclusion

Access to the metaverse is not universally equal. **Economic, technological,** and **social barriers** present significant challenges to the full inclusion of many individuals. However, efforts are being made to reduce these barriers and create more **inclusive, accessible,** and **equitable** virtual environments. By addressing issues such as affordability, internet access, and the needs of marginalized groups, the metaverse has the potential to become a space where everyone can participate, create, and connect—regardless of their background or resources.

As the metaverse continues to evolve, ensuring equal access will be crucial to making it a truly **inclusive** and **accessible** digital frontier. Developers, platform creators, and the broader virtual world community must continue to prioritize **diversity**, **inclusivity**, and **accessibility** to ensure that the metaverse can live up to its promise of a digital space for all.

CHAPTER 11

THE LEGAL LANDSCAPE: UNDERSTANDING THE METAVERSE'S LEGAL FRAMEWORK

Overview of Existing Laws That Apply to Virtual Spaces

As virtual spaces like the metaverse continue to grow, the need to understand the **legal framework** surrounding these digital environments becomes increasingly important. Traditional laws designed for the physical world are often not sufficient to address the unique challenges posed by virtual spaces. However, existing legal structures—such as **intellectual property laws, contract law, privacy regulations**, and **cybersecurity laws**—already provide some legal foundation for virtual interactions. Let's examine the key areas where existing laws apply to virtual worlds.

1. **Intellectual Property Laws**: **Intellectual property (IP) laws** play a critical role in protecting the creative work and digital assets that exist within the metaverse. Virtual goods, including avatars, clothing, virtual land, and digital art, may be subject to

97

copyright, trademark, and patent laws, depending on the nature of the item and its use within the virtual environment.

- o **Copyright**: Copyright laws protect the original creation of works like digital art, software, and music. In virtual worlds, creators of avatars, virtual items, and environments can assert their **copyright** over the content they create. Similarly, users who design and share content within these worlds can claim ownership over their creations.

  - ▪ **Example**: In **Second Life**, users can design virtual clothes and 3D models, which are protected under copyright law. This protection ensures that creators can prevent others from using their designs without permission.

- o **Trademarks**: Brands operating in the metaverse are also protected by **trademark** laws. If a brand is offering virtual products or hosting events in a virtual space, its name, logo, and other branding elements can be protected under trademark law. Additionally, the use of an established brand's trademark in virtual spaces without permission can lead to infringement claims.

  - ▪ **Example**: When virtual items and experiences are branded with established names (such as **Gucci** or **Nike**), they must ensure that the use of their brand is not infringing on existing trademark rights or misleading consumers.

2. **Contract** **Law**: Contract law is vital in virtual worlds, especially when it comes to **terms of service** (ToS), **end-user license agreements** (EULAs), and other agreements between users and platform operators. Virtual worlds often require users to agree to ToS or EULAs, which set the rules for participating in these environments. These agreements govern user behavior, dispute resolution, ownership rights, and platform liability.

   o **Example**: In **Fortnite**, users must agree to the game's ToS and EULA before participating. These agreements typically include clauses about **user-generated content** ownership, the platform's right to moderate user behavior, and the resolution of disputes through arbitration instead of court.

3. **Privacy and Data Protection Laws**: As users interact within the metaverse, vast amounts of personal data are collected, including sensitive information like biometric data (in VR spaces), financial information (for in-game purchases), and behavioral data (such as movement and preferences). Given the high

99

volume of data generated in virtual environments, **privacy laws** are increasingly important.

- o **General Data Protection Regulation (GDPR)**: The **GDPR** is a regulation in the European Union (EU) that establishes strict rules around data protection and privacy. It applies to platforms operating in the EU or targeting EU users. The GDPR provides individuals with control over their personal data, requiring platforms to obtain explicit consent for data collection, notify users of breaches, and give them the ability to access and delete their personal information.

- o **Example**: If a virtual platform like **VRChat** collects biometric data (such as voice or motion data) to improve user interaction, it must comply with privacy regulations like the GDPR to ensure that this sensitive data is stored securely and only used with user consent.

4. **Cybersecurity   Laws**: **Cybersecurity** is a growing concern as virtual worlds become more integrated with real-world activities. Laws that govern cybersecurity address the **protection of users' personal information**, the **prevention of hacking**, and the **security of virtual assets**. These laws aim to ensure that virtual spaces are safe from breaches, fraud, and malicious activity.

- o **Example**: In the case of **blockchain-based virtual worlds** like **Decentraland** or **The Sandbox**, users own virtual land and assets represented as NFTs. Cybersecurity laws regulate the protection of these digital assets to prevent hacking, fraud, or unauthorized access. If a user's virtual land or assets are stolen due to inadequate cybersecurity measures, the platform could be held liable for failing to protect its users' assets.

5. **Consumer Protection Laws**: As virtual worlds become more commercialized, **consumer protection** laws play a vital role in ensuring fair business practices and preventing exploitation. These laws govern the rights of consumers purchasing virtual goods, services, or experiences, ensuring that they receive what they were promised and that their purchases are not misleading or fraudulent.

   - o **Example**: If a user in **Roblox** purchases virtual items (such as clothing or game passes), consumer protection laws require that the platform delivers what was advertised. If the item is defective or fails to meet expectations, the platform may be required to offer a refund or other remedy.

How Legal Systems Are Adapting to Digital Environments

As virtual worlds grow in complexity, traditional legal systems are evolving to address the unique challenges posed by these digital environments. Governments and legal systems around the world are developing new regulations and frameworks that specifically target the emerging issues within virtual spaces.

1. **New Laws for Virtual Worlds**: While existing laws provide a foundation for regulating virtual worlds, many jurisdictions are beginning to introduce **new laws and regulations** tailored to the unique characteristics of the metaverse. These new laws often focus on **virtual asset ownership**, **digital rights**, **platform governance**, and **user safety**.

   o **Example**: In the United States, the **Virtual Digital Asset Regulation** Act (introduced in 2021) aims to regulate virtual assets like NFTs and cryptocurrency, ensuring consumer protection and financial stability in virtual markets.

   o **Example**: In South Korea, **Virtual Asset Regulation** requires companies in virtual worlds that deal with real-world transactions (such as selling virtual goods for real money) to comply with anti-money laundering laws and financial transparency regulations.

2. **International Cooperation and Harmonization**: Because the metaverse operates on a global scale, legal issues that arise in virtual spaces often cross international borders. To address this, **international cooperation** among governments and regulatory bodies is essential. Many countries are now collaborating to harmonize laws related to the metaverse, particularly in areas like **intellectual property, data protection**, and **cybersecurity**.

   o **Example**: The **World Intellectual Property Organization (WIPO)** is exploring how international intellectual property laws can be applied to virtual worlds, particularly in relation to **NFTs** and **copyright protection** for virtual assets.

   o **Example**: The **European Union** is working on a **Digital Markets Act** and **Digital Services Act**, which aim to regulate large digital platforms and ensure that virtual spaces are not monopolized by a few companies, creating a fair and competitive environment for users and businesses alike.

3. **Jurisdictional   Challenges**: One of the most difficult aspects of applying traditional legal frameworks to the metaverse is the question of **jurisdiction**—where legal authority lies when a dispute arises in a virtual space. Since virtual worlds can span

multiple countries, it can be unclear which country's laws apply to users from different parts of the world, especially when incidents like harassment, intellectual property theft, or fraud occur.

- o **Example**: A user in **Decentraland** who is located in Canada might purchase virtual land that is represented as an NFT. If the user feels that their land was unfairly taken or their intellectual property rights were violated, which country's laws govern the dispute? Jurisdictional issues like this one are still evolving and remain a key challenge for legal systems.

4. **Blockchain and Smart Contracts**: **Blockchain technology** and **smart contracts** are central to many metaverse platforms, enabling decentralized ownership and automated transactions. These technologies present both opportunities and challenges for legal systems.

- o **Smart Contracts**: Smart contracts are self-executing contracts with the terms of the agreement directly written into code. While they offer efficiency and transparency, they also pose challenges in terms of enforcement and interpretation. Legal systems must determine how to **enforce** these contracts in cases of disputes, especially when they involve international users or cross-border transactions.

- o **Example**: In **NFT transactions**, smart contracts govern the sale and transfer of digital assets. However, if a buyer claims that the contract was violated, how will the legal system handle the enforcement of a smart contract's terms, especially when the buyer and seller are in different countries?

Conclusion

As the metaverse grows into an integral part of digital life, the legal landscape surrounding virtual spaces will continue to evolve. Existing laws, such as those concerning intellectual property, contract law, privacy, and cybersecurity, offer a foundation for regulating virtual worlds, but new challenges are emerging that require tailored legal frameworks. International cooperation, jurisdictional clarity, and the regulation of digital assets and smart contracts will be key to managing the metaverse's legal complexities.

Legal systems must adapt to ensure that the metaverse is not only innovative and accessible but also fair, secure, and protective of users' rights. The future of digital spaces depends on creating a legal environment that balances freedom and creativity with accountability and protection. As virtual worlds continue to develop, so too must the laws that govern them, ensuring a safe, equitable, and transparent space for all participants.

CHAPTER 12

INTELLECTUAL PROPERTY IN THE METAVERSE: PROTECTING YOUR CREATIONS

Copyright, Trademarks, and Patents in Virtual Environments

As virtual worlds in the metaverse continue to expand, the importance of **intellectual property (IP)** becomes increasingly significant. In these immersive digital environments, users and creators are constantly producing **virtual assets**, from digital art and clothing to entire virtual environments and games. As in the physical world, **intellectual property laws**—such as **copyright**, **trademarks**, and **patents**—are essential to protecting the rights of creators and ensuring that their work is not exploited without permission. However, these laws, originally designed for physical goods, must now be adapted to address the unique nature of digital creations.

1. **Copyright in the Metaverse**:
    Copyright protects original works of authorship, such as literary, artistic, and musical creations. In the metaverse, this can include virtual art, 3D models, music, avatars, and

other user-generated content (UGC). If a creator develops a piece of virtual art or designs a new game asset, that creation is protected by copyright law, which grants the creator exclusive rights to reproduce, distribute, and display the work.

- o **Digital Art**: In virtual worlds, digital art is one of the most prevalent forms of creation. Artists who design virtual clothing, avatars, and landscapes often assert their copyright over these creations to prevent others from using or copying their work without permission.

  - **Example**: An artist who designs a virtual painting in **Decentraland** or **Cryptovoxels** can claim copyright over that artwork. Copyright law ensures that they retain the exclusive right to reproduce, distribute, and sell the digital artwork.

- o **Music and Sound**: Music and sound effects created for virtual spaces or virtual performances are also protected by copyright. In the metaverse, musicians may create virtual soundtracks for games or performances, which are protected by copyright law, giving them the right to control how the music is used.

- **Example**: In platforms like **Second Life**, musicians can sell virtual performances or soundtracks, and their intellectual property rights are protected by copyright, which prevents others from distributing or profiting from their music without authorization.

2. **Trademarks in the Metaverse**: **Trademarks** are used to protect brand names, logos, slogans, and other distinctive signs that distinguish products or services. In the metaverse, trademarks help companies and creators protect their brand identities, ensuring that others cannot use their logos or names in ways that could cause confusion or harm the brand's reputation.

   o **Branding in Virtual Spaces**: As more companies and creators move into virtual environments, **trademark protection** is essential to safeguard their brand identity. For instance, brands like **Nike**, **Gucci**, and **Adidas** have begun selling virtual clothing and accessories in the metaverse. The use of their logos and branding is protected by trademark law, which prevents unauthorized use in virtual spaces.

      - **Example**: If a user in **Roblox** designs a virtual hoodie with the Nike swoosh

109

logo, it would infringe upon Nike's trademark, and the company could pursue legal action to protect its brand. Similarly, virtual spaces hosting branded events or virtual products must be careful not to infringe on trademarks by using logos or names without permission.

3. **Patents in the Metaverse**: **Patents** protect inventions or technological innovations. In the context of the metaverse, patents can cover **software algorithms**, **virtual reality hardware**, or **unique technological processes** used to create virtual environments. Innovators who develop new technologies for virtual spaces or enhance existing VR/AR systems may seek patent protection to prevent others from copying their inventions.

   o **Virtual Reality Hardware**: Companies that create specialized hardware for virtual reality, such as VR headsets, motion sensors, or haptic feedback systems, can patent these innovations to prevent competitors from producing similar products without permission.

      ▪ **Example: Oculus** (a subsidiary of Meta) has patented several innovations related to its VR headsets, such as motion-tracking systems and hardware design.

These patents prevent other companies from copying the technology and ensure that Oculus retains a competitive edge in the virtual reality market.

Case Studies: Digital Art, NFTs, and Virtual Assets

As the metaverse grows, the intersection of **intellectual property** and virtual assets like **digital art, NFTs (Non-Fungible Tokens),** and **virtual goods** has created new challenges and opportunities for creators. Below, we explore case studies that highlight how intellectual property laws apply in the context of digital art, NFTs, and virtual assets.

1. **Digital   Art   in   the   Metaverse**: Digital art has gained significant attention in the metaverse due to the rise of **NFTs** (Non-Fungible Tokens). Artists are now able to create unique, digital artworks that can be bought, sold, and traded as NFTs, representing ownership of a one-of-a-kind piece of art on the blockchain.

    o **Example**: One of the most famous examples of digital art in the metaverse is the sale of **Beeple's** digital artwork "Everydays: The First 5000 Days." This piece of art was sold as an NFT for **$69 million** at a Christie's auction in 2021,

111

highlighting the growing importance of digital art in the virtual world. The copyright for Beeple's work remains with the artist, but the buyer of the NFT holds ownership of the tokenized artwork and has the right to resell it.

- o **Copyright and NFTs**: When a digital artwork is sold as an NFT, the buyer typically does not automatically gain copyright over the artwork itself. Instead, they own the NFT, which represents the **tokenized version** of the artwork. The artist retains copyright, meaning they can still reproduce or license the artwork to other parties, but the NFT owner can resell or display the NFT as they choose.

2. **NFTs and Virtual Assets**: NFTs are playing a major role in the **ownership and trade** of virtual assets in the metaverse, from virtual land and properties to in-game items like weapons, skins, and clothing. NFTs offer a solution to the challenge of **digital scarcity**—by proving the ownership of a unique digital asset, NFTs provide value and exclusivity to virtual items.

- o **Example**: Platforms like **Decentraland** and **The Sandbox** sell virtual land and assets as NFTs, allowing users to buy, sell, and trade parcels of land within these metaverse environments. Users can buy virtual properties, build on them, and even monetize them, knowing that their ownership is secured through the blockchain and protected by intellectual property rights.

- o **Case Study: The Sale of Virtual Land**: In **Decentraland**, virtual land is bought and sold as NFTs, allowing users to create virtual stores, galleries, or experiences. In 2021, a parcel of virtual land in Decentraland sold for **$2.4 million**, underscoring the growing importance of virtual assets in the metaverse economy.

3. **Virtual Goods and In-Game Assets**: In many virtual worlds, users create and purchase **virtual goods**—such as avatar clothing, in-game items, and accessories—that exist only within the game. These items often have real-world value and can be bought, sold, and traded between players, sometimes for significant amounts of money. However, questions surrounding the ownership and rights to these items remain complex.

- o **Example**: In **World of Warcraft**, players buy and sell **in-game items** (such as rare weapons or mounts) within the game, and some of these items can be traded on third-party platforms for real-world money. Although the virtual items have value within the game, players do not actually own them in the traditional sense; the game publisher, Blizzard Entertainment, retains control

113

over the items, and players are subject to the platform's terms of service.

- ○ **Copyright and Licensing**: When players create or modify virtual items (such as avatars or custom skins), those creations may be protected by copyright. However, the terms of service in many virtual worlds often grant platform owners the **right to use, modify, or delete** user-created content. This creates a complicated situation where players may feel ownership over their creations, but the platform holds the ultimate control over how they are used and monetized.

Conclusion

As the metaverse continues to evolve, **intellectual property (IP)** law plays a crucial role in protecting the rights of creators, users, and businesses within virtual spaces. Whether it's **copyright** for digital art, **trademarks** for brands, or **patents** for new technologies, existing laws provide the framework for addressing the unique challenges of the metaverse. The advent of **NFTs** has further complicated IP law, introducing new opportunities for creators to monetize their digital work while also raising questions about ownership, licensing, and infringement.

As virtual worlds continue to grow and commercialize, understanding how **intellectual property** is applied—and how legal systems are adapting to new technologies—is essential for creators and participants in the metaverse. By navigating these laws carefully, individuals can protect their virtual creations, avoid legal disputes, and ensure that their work is respected and properly compensated in these emerging digital environments.

CHAPTER 13

DIGITAL THEFT: HACKING, SCAMS, AND FRAUD IN VIRTUAL WORLDS

The Rise of Cybercrime in the Metaverse

As the metaverse continues to evolve and grow in both complexity and popularity, **cybercrime** has become a significant concern for users, creators, and platform operators. Just as the physical world is susceptible to theft, fraud, and scams, virtual environments are also prime targets for various forms of digital theft. With the rise of valuable **virtual assets**, **cryptocurrency**, and **NFTs (Non-Fungible Tokens)**, cybercriminals are increasingly exploiting weaknesses in digital security to profit from their illicit activities. The unique nature of the metaverse—blending gaming, commerce, and social interaction—has given rise to novel forms of **digital crime**, including hacking, scams, and fraud.

1. **Hacking in the Metaverse**: **Hacking** in virtual worlds often involves unauthorized access to user accounts, virtual assets, or entire platforms. Cybercriminals exploit vulnerabilities in the software,

network, or security protocols of virtual environments to steal assets, cause disruption, or manipulate the system for malicious purposes.

- o **Account Hacking**: One of the most common forms of hacking in the metaverse involves **account hijacking**, where cybercriminals gain access to a user's account and steal their virtual assets, such as NFTs, cryptocurrency, or in-game items. This is particularly prevalent in environments where users hold valuable items that can be resold or traded.

  - **Example**: In **Second Life**, users who own virtual real estate, digital art, or in-game items can be targeted by hackers who steal their login credentials. Once the hacker gains access, they can sell or transfer these assets to other accounts, often without the original owner's knowledge.

- o **Platform Hacking**: In addition to targeting individual accounts, hackers may also attack the underlying platform or virtual world itself. This can involve exploiting security flaws in the platform's servers, allowing hackers to steal sensitive data, manipulate the virtual economy, or disrupt the operation of the platform.

- **Example**: In 2021, a vulnerability in **Axie Infinity**, a blockchain-based game, was exploited by hackers who stole over **$600 million** worth of cryptocurrency. The breach was traced to a flaw in the game's security infrastructure, highlighting the vulnerability of blockchain-based virtual worlds to sophisticated hacking attacks.

2. **Scams in Virtual Worlds**: As virtual worlds become increasingly integrated with real-world commerce, **scams** have proliferated within these environments. These scams often involve misleading or fraudulent activities designed to deceive users into parting with their virtual goods, cryptocurrency, or personal information. Virtual scams can take many forms, ranging from fake NFT sales to phishing attacks targeting users' credentials.

   o **Phishing Scams**: Phishing involves tricking users into revealing personal information, such as usernames, passwords, or credit card details. Cybercriminals often impersonate trusted platform operators or creators to gain access to sensitive information. These scams are particularly prevalent in virtual environments where users may be interacting with strangers and may not be as cautious about online security.

- **Example**: In **Decentraland** or **The Sandbox**, scammers may create fake websites or social media accounts that impersonate popular creators or platforms, tricking users into sending cryptocurrency or NFTs to fraudulent wallets. Once the user sends the digital assets, they are gone, and the scammer vanishes with the funds.

- **Fake NFT Sales**: With the explosion of NFTs as a popular asset class in the metaverse, many users are becoming increasingly aware of potential scams involving fake NFT sales. These scams often involve scammers selling **stolen** or **counterfeit NFTs** that appear legitimate. Unsuspecting buyers may be led to believe they are purchasing rare or exclusive items, only to discover later that the assets are fake or fraudulent.

  - **Example**: In 2021, a **counterfeit NFT scam** involved fake digital art being sold as legitimate works by well-known artists. Scammers used manipulated metadata and fake proofs of ownership to

119

convince buyers to purchase NFTs that had no value or authenticity.

3. **Fraud in Virtual Worlds**: **Fraud** in the metaverse is a broader issue that encompasses both individual scams and larger-scale fraudulent activities, such as fraudulent virtual asset sales, fake investment schemes, and financial fraud. With the growth of virtual currencies and blockchain technology, there is an increasing number of fraudsters attempting to exploit the decentralized nature of virtual worlds to deceive users.

- **Investment Scams**: As virtual assets like NFTs and cryptocurrency gain value, fraudsters often create fake investment opportunities or **Ponzi schemes** to lure users into investing in fraudulent projects or virtual assets that don't exist. These scams can promise high returns, only to disappear with the investors' funds.

  - **Example**: A scammer might advertise an NFT or cryptocurrency investment opportunity in a virtual world like **Roblox**, promising players exclusive returns or early access to a valuable collection. Once users invest, the scammer vanishes, leaving the users with nothing.

o **Asset Fraud**: Another form of fraud in virtual worlds involves fraudulent sales or manipulation of virtual assets, such as real estate, rare in-game items, or digital collectibles. Users may be led to believe that they are purchasing an item or asset with significant value, only to find that the transaction is fraudulent, and the asset is worthless or non-existent.

- **Example**: In **Decentraland**, users have reported buying virtual land parcels that were misrepresented as having valuable, exclusive content. After the transaction, they discover that the land is not as advertised, or it has no value at all in the virtual economy.

Legal and Ethical Approaches to Combatting Digital Theft

As digital theft continues to pose significant challenges to the metaverse, both **legal** and **ethical** frameworks must be put in place to protect users and prevent cybercrime. While existing laws related to cybercrime, intellectual property, and consumer protection provide some level of protection, they must evolve to meet the unique demands of virtual spaces.

1. **Legal Approaches to Digital Theft**: **Legal systems** worldwide are beginning to adapt to the rise of cybercrime in virtual worlds. Many countries have established or are updating laws to address crimes such as **hacking, fraud**, and **theft of digital assets**. These laws are increasingly being applied to virtual worlds and digital environments, especially those that involve financial transactions, virtual currencies, and NFTs.

   o **Cybersecurity Laws**: Governments are enacting stricter **cybersecurity laws** to ensure that platforms in the metaverse take adequate measures to protect user data and digital assets. These laws require platforms to implement strong security protocols and prevent unauthorized access to users' personal information and virtual assets.

      ▪ **Example**: In the United States, the **Computer Fraud and Abuse Act (CFAA)** provides a framework for prosecuting cybercrimes, including hacking and unauthorized access to computer systems. This law could be applied to virtual worlds where hackers steal digital assets or disrupt the functioning of platforms.

- o **Consumer Protection**: Legal protections for consumers in virtual worlds are increasingly important, especially as scams and fraudulent activities rise. **Consumer protection laws** ensure that users are not misled by fraudulent schemes, and that they have the ability to seek compensation or legal recourse in cases of theft or fraud.

  - **Example**: The **Federal Trade Commission (FTC)** in the United States has the authority to regulate and penalize fraudulent schemes in digital spaces. This includes fraud related to NFTs, virtual currencies, and online gaming.

2. **Ethical Approaches to Combatting Digital Theft**: While legal frameworks are essential in addressing digital theft, **ethical approaches** also play a crucial role in creating safe, trustworthy virtual environments. Developers, platforms, and community members all have a role to play in upholding ethical standards and fostering a culture of **integrity, transparency**, and **respect** in virtual worlds.

   - o **Platform Responsibility**: Virtual platforms must take **responsibility** for securing user data and protecting users from scams, hacking, and fraud. This includes implementing **robust verification** systems, **anti-fraud tools**, and **reporting mechanisms** to help prevent and address cybercrime.

- **Example**: **Roblox** has implemented a **moderation system** to detect and block scams, including fake virtual item listings and phishing attempts. They also educate users about the dangers of scams and provide tools to report suspicious activity.

o **Community Standards and Self-Regulation**: In addition to platform-wide security measures, virtual world communities can take an active role in preventing theft and fraud through **self-regulation**. This includes creating and enforcing community guidelines that prohibit scams, fraudulent activity, and other unethical behaviors. By fostering an environment of trust and mutual respect, communities can help deter digital theft.

- **Example**: **Discord** servers often have community moderators who enforce rules against fraudulent activity, including fake NFT sales and phishing attempts. Community members are encouraged to report suspicious behavior and collaborate to prevent scams within the server.

3. **User Education and Awareness**: Educating users about the risks of **cybercrime**, including hacking, scams, and fraud, is crucial in preventing digital theft. Many users, particularly those who are new to virtual worlds, may not be fully aware of the potential dangers they face when engaging in online transactions or sharing personal information.

   o **Example**: Many metaverse platforms, such as **Decentraland** and **VRChat**, provide educational resources and warnings about potential scams, offering advice on how to identify fraudulent schemes and how to protect personal assets.

Conclusion

Digital theft, including hacking, scams, and fraud, is a growing concern in the metaverse. As virtual worlds become increasingly integrated with real-world commerce and social interactions, cybercrime continues to evolve in complexity. To combat these threats, both **legal** and **ethical** approaches are needed. Legal systems must adapt to ensure that digital theft is properly addressed, while platform creators, developers, and communities must uphold ethical standards to protect users and foster trust.

By improving security, implementing transparent practices, and educating users, the metaverse can become a safer, more reliable space for creativity, commerce, and social interaction. As the digital world continues to expand, it is crucial that we develop stronger frameworks—both legal and ethical—to safeguard the interests of all participants.

CHAPTER 14

DATA PRIVACY AND SECURITY: PROTECTING USERS IN THE METAVERSE

How Data Is Collected, Shared, and Stored

In the metaverse, **data privacy** and **security** are critical issues. As users navigate virtual worlds, their actions, interactions, and personal information generate vast amounts of data. This data can be used to enhance the user experience, create targeted advertising, or improve the functionality of virtual platforms. However, it also raises significant concerns about how this data is **collected**, **shared**, and **stored**, and who has access to it. Understanding these processes is crucial to maintaining a safe and ethical virtual environment.

1. **Data Collection in the Metaverse**: The process of **data collection** begins the moment users enter virtual spaces. Platforms in the metaverse gather information through various means, such as user profiles, in-game actions, voice communications, and even biometric data. This information is then used for a variety

of purposes, from improving user experience to enabling targeted advertising.

- o **User Profiles**: When users sign up for metaverse platforms, they often create detailed profiles, providing personal information such as their name, email address, and preferences. This data is typically collected and stored by the platform, and it forms the foundation of the user's experience within the virtual world.

  - **Example**: In platforms like **VRChat**, users create profiles that include information about their avatar, preferences, and interests. This data is used to personalize their virtual experience, suggesting new spaces or friends based on their activity.

- o **Behavioral Data**: Virtual platforms also collect **behavioral data**—such as users' interactions with other avatars, the virtual environments they explore, and their purchase history. This data allows platforms to tailor content, improve gameplay, and target specific advertisements to users.

  - **Example**: In **Roblox**, developers can track players' actions within the game, such as the types of games they play, how often they play, and which items they purchase. This data helps game creators customize the gameplay experience and increase engagement.

o **Biometric Data**: Some platforms in the metaverse, especially those utilizing **virtual reality (VR)** or **augmented reality (AR)**, can collect **biometric data**. This includes information like facial expressions, body movements, and even eye tracking, all of which can be used to create more immersive experiences. Biometric data is often used to enhance user interaction, making virtual spaces feel more lifelike.

   ▪ **Example**: **VRChat** uses eye-tracking and facial expression recognition to make avatars more expressive and realistic. However, this type of data collection also raises concerns about privacy, as it involves capturing sensitive physical attributes of users.

2. **Data Sharing in the Metaverse**: Once data is collected, it may be shared with third parties, including advertisers, business partners, or other users. How data is shared can vary significantly from platform to platform, but many virtual environments use the data

129

they collect to drive monetization efforts through targeted advertising or content recommendations.

- ○ **Advertisers and Marketers**: Virtual platforms often use collected data to create **targeted advertising**, ensuring that users are shown products or services that align with their interests and behavior. This can include in-game advertisements, personalized content, or even product placements within virtual environments.

    - ▪ **Example**: In **Fortnite**, players may encounter advertisements or product placements for real-world brands, such as Nike or Coca-Cola, seamlessly integrated into the virtual world. The targeting of these ads is made possible by user data collected from the platform, ensuring that the ads are relevant to the player's interests and preferences.

- ○ **Social Sharing**: Many virtual platforms allow users to **share data** with others, such as their activity logs, virtual assets, or social interactions. While this can help create a more connected and social experience, it also raises questions about **who controls the data** and how it can be used by others within the platform.

130

○ **Example: Second Life** allows users to create, share, and trade digital assets like virtual land and clothing, which can be freely transferred between users. This creates a complex web of data sharing that raises concerns about intellectual property and privacy, especially when digital assets are linked to real-world currency.

3. **Data Storage in the Metaverse**: The storage of data in the metaverse can involve cloud-based solutions, decentralized networks, or traditional servers, depending on the platform. The way data is stored affects how **secure** and **accessible** it is to both the platform operators and third parties.

○ **Centralized vs. Decentralized Storage**: In **centralized** platforms, data is stored on company-owned servers, which means that the platform has complete control over how the data is used, accessed, and protected. On the other hand, **decentralized** platforms use blockchain or distributed ledger technologies to store data, making it more transparent but also more difficult to regulate or control.

○ **Example: Decentraland** uses blockchain technology to store ownership information about virtual land and assets, ensuring transparency and decentralization. However, this also means that

131

users have a more permanent record of their activities and purchases on the blockchain, which could raise concerns about data permanence and privacy.

The Ethics of Surveillance, Consent, and Privacy Within Virtual Spaces

As virtual worlds become more embedded in daily life, the **ethical implications** of data collection, surveillance, and privacy become increasingly important. How data is gathered, who has access to it, and how it is used, are critical questions for maintaining trust and integrity within the metaverse. These concerns touch on issues of **surveillance**, **user consent**, and **the right to privacy**, each of which must be carefully considered to create ethical virtual environments.

1. **Surveillance in the Metaverse**: In virtual spaces, **surveillance** refers to the monitoring of users' activities, behaviors, and interactions. While surveillance can help improve the user experience by offering personalized content and enhancing security, it also raises ethical concerns about users being constantly monitored.

   o **Example**: Some platforms, like **VRChat**, collect **real-time data** on users' movements, facial expressions, and social interactions. While this data is used to enhance the experience (making avatars more expressive), it also means that users are being constantly monitored by the platform. The more immersive and interactive the experience, the greater the potential for surveillance, which can create a sense of discomfort or distrust among users.

- o **Ethical Concerns**: The ethical dilemma arises when users are unaware of the extent to which they are being monitored or when data is used for purposes they did not explicitly consent to. The use of surveillance for profit—such as targeted ads or data reselling—raises concerns about **data exploitation** and the **violation of user autonomy**.

2. **Consent in Virtual Spaces**: **User consent** is a cornerstone of ethical data collection. For virtual worlds to respect users' privacy, they must ensure that users understand what data is being collected, how it will be used, and who will have access to it. Clear **informed consent** is necessary to maintain trust and prevent exploitation.

- o **Example**: When users sign up for platforms like **Second Life** or **Horizon Worlds**, they are often required to accept terms of service that outline the

133

platform's data collection practices. However, these terms are often long, complex, and difficult for the average user to fully understand. Without **informed consent**, users may unknowingly give permission for their personal data to be used in ways they didn't anticipate.

- o **Ethical Issues**: The ethical issue with consent arises when platforms do not make it clear what data they are collecting or when the consent process is misleading. **Opt-in vs. opt-out** systems—where users must choose to participate in data collection or advertising—can lead to ethical issues if users are unknowingly enrolled in data-sharing programs.

3. **Privacy in the Metaverse**: **Privacy** in virtual worlds is a delicate balance between user autonomy and platform functionality. As virtual environments collect and store vast amounts of data, including sensitive personal information, it is essential that these platforms implement strong **privacy protections** to safeguard users' rights.

- o **Data Protection Regulations**: Various laws and regulations, such as the **General Data Protection Regulation (GDPR)** in the European Union, are designed to protect users' privacy and give them control over their personal data. These regulations ensure that platforms must be transparent about data collection, offer users the ability to access and delete their data, and prevent misuse of that data.

- **Example**: A platform like **Roblox** must comply with privacy laws such as the **Children's Online Privacy Protection Act (COPPA)** when collecting data from minors. This law ensures that platforms collecting information from children under 13 must obtain parental consent and protect children's data from being exploited.

o **Ethical Dilemmas**: Privacy concerns also arise when users' data is used for purposes beyond the user's control or consent, such as selling data to third-party marketers or creating detailed digital profiles for manipulation. For example, **behavioral tracking** of users' movements, interactions, or purchases within virtual worlds can be exploited to predict or influence their future behavior in ways that may not be ethical or transparent.

Conclusion

Data privacy and security are critical components of maintaining trust and integrity in the metaverse. As virtual worlds become increasingly immersive, the **collection, sharing,** and **storage** of personal data will continue to raise significant ethical and legal concerns. Platforms must balance the need to collect data for personalization and functionality with the imperative to protect users' privacy and ensure **informed consent**.

Addressing the **ethics of surveillance, data consent,** and **privacy** will be key to the future of the metaverse. By implementing strong privacy protections, ensuring transparency in data collection practices, and fostering ethical guidelines for data use, the metaverse can evolve into a space that respects users' rights and encourages safe, inclusive participation for all.

CHAPTER 15

CONTRACT LAW AND TRANSACTIONS IN THE METAVERSE

Legal Contracts in Virtual Environments: Buying and Selling Virtual Goods

As the metaverse continues to expand, **contract law** plays an essential role in regulating transactions, particularly the buying and selling of **virtual goods**. These goods—whether virtual land, avatars, in-game items, or NFTs—represent valuable assets within digital environments and, as such, require legal frameworks to ensure that the parties involved in transactions understand their rights and obligations. Legal contracts in virtual spaces help define the terms of these transactions, protect both buyers and sellers, and ensure that the virtual economy operates fairly and transparently.

1. **Contract Formation in the Metaverse**: **Contracts** in virtual environments are often formed when a user agrees to a platform's **Terms of Service (ToS)** or an **End-User License Agreement (EULA)**. These

agreements serve as the foundation for transactions, outlining the rights and responsibilities of the users as they engage in buying, selling, or trading virtual goods.

- o **Example**: In **Decentraland**, users purchase virtual real estate using cryptocurrency (such as **MANA** tokens). When they make such purchases, they typically agree to the platform's ToS, which acts as a **contract** governing the transaction. These terms include rules about virtual land ownership, trading, and what users can and cannot do with the purchased assets.

- o **EULAs and Ownership Rights**: Virtual platforms often employ **EULAs** to outline the terms under which users can buy or sell virtual goods. For example, a user buying an in-game item like a skin in **Fortnite** is agreeing to an EULA that specifies that they are purchasing a **license** to use the item, not outright ownership. This distinction between **ownership** and **license** is critical in the context of virtual goods and affects how these assets can be traded or resold.

2. **Virtual Goods and Digital Assets**: Virtual goods and **digital assets**—such as **NFTs (Non-Fungible Tokens)**—are often the subject of transactions within virtual environments. While these digital assets may appear similar to traditional goods, they have unique

characteristics, such as being **unique, digital, and sometimes tied to cryptocurrency**, making them subject to different legal considerations.

- o **Example**: **NFTs** in the metaverse, such as virtual art or collectible items, are typically bought and sold through blockchain transactions. These transactions are verified and recorded on a **decentralized ledger**, ensuring transparency and security. The legal framework for NFTs requires clarity regarding the **ownership, transferability**, and **intellectual property rights** associated with these digital assets.

- o **Example**: In **Roblox**, users purchase and sell virtual clothing and accessories for avatars, often using the in-game currency **Robux**. The virtual goods in Roblox are subject to Roblox's ToS, which outlines the rules for buying, selling, and trading in-game items. The legal relationship is governed by Roblox's rules, and these purchases are typically considered **licenses** to use the virtual goods within the platform, not full ownership.

3. **Smart Contracts and Automation**: One of the most significant technological advancements in virtual transactions is the use of **smart contracts**. These are self-executing contracts with the terms of the agreement directly written into code, which automatically

execute when predefined conditions are met. Smart contracts are commonly used in blockchain-based platforms and NFTs to facilitate secure and transparent transactions without the need for intermediaries.

- o **Example**: In **Ethereum-based platforms** like **OpenSea**, where users buy and sell NFTs, smart contracts ensure that when a buyer purchases an NFT, the payment is automatically transferred to the seller, and the NFT is transferred to the buyer's wallet. These contracts help ensure that the transaction is transparent, secure, and executed according to the terms agreed upon by both parties.

- o **Example**: On platforms like **Decentraland** or **The Sandbox**, when users buy virtual land or digital assets, smart contracts automatically verify and enforce the sale terms, such as ownership transfer and payment. This eliminates the need for a middleman and ensures the transaction is completed according to the agreed-upon terms.

Consumer Protection, Fraud, and Dispute Resolution

While the metaverse presents exciting opportunities for digital commerce, it also raises significant concerns about **consumer**

protection, **fraud**, and **dispute resolution**. The virtual economy, especially with the rise of NFTs and virtual assets, can be prone to scams, fraud, and unclear transaction terms. Legal systems and platform operators must address these challenges to protect users and ensure fair practices.

1. **Consumer Protection in Virtual Transactions**: **Consumer protection laws** are designed to safeguard the rights of users when engaging in transactions, ensuring that they are not misled, defrauded, or taken advantage of. In the metaverse, these protections need to be adapted to address the unique nature of virtual goods and services, which can sometimes be intangible or speculative.

   o **Transparency in Transactions**: Virtual platforms must ensure that consumers are fully informed about the nature of the goods or services they are purchasing. This includes clear disclosures about **pricing, ownership rights**, and **the value of digital assets**.

      ▪ **Example**: In **Axie Infinity**, a game where users can buy and sell virtual creatures (Axies), players must be made aware of the potential financial risks of investing in these virtual assets, as the value of Axies can fluctuate significantly. Clear terms about what users are purchasing—whether it's a

141

game asset, an NFT, or a digital collectible—must be outlined in the platform's terms and agreements.

- ○ **Refunds and Returns**: One of the biggest challenges in virtual commerce is the issue of refunds and returns. Since virtual goods are often non-tangible and **non-refundable**, platforms must clearly define their policies on these matters to ensure users know what to expect if a purchase goes wrong.

  - **Example**: If a user purchases an NFT from a marketplace like **OpenSea**, they are typically not entitled to a refund, as the transaction is final and irreversible. However, users should be informed of this before making the purchase to avoid confusion or dissatisfaction.

2. **Fraud and Scams**: Fraudulent activities are a growing concern in virtual spaces, particularly as the financial stakes in digital assets rise. **Fraud** in the metaverse can include fake NFT sales, counterfeit virtual goods, phishing scams, and more. To protect users, platforms must implement strong anti-fraud measures and work with legal authorities to address violations.

o **Phishing and Scams**: Scammers in virtual environments often create fake websites or impersonate legitimate entities to trick users into revealing sensitive information, such as usernames, passwords, or cryptocurrency wallet keys. These scams are especially prevalent in the NFT and cryptocurrency sectors of the metaverse.

- **Example**: A scammer might create a **fake NFT auction** on a platform like **Rarible** to lure users into purchasing counterfeit digital art or transferring cryptocurrency to a fraudulent wallet. Users must be vigilant and only engage with verified, trusted platforms to avoid falling victim to these types of scams.

o **Counterfeit Virtual Goods**: Similar to physical-world counterfeit goods, virtual platforms may face issues with counterfeit digital assets, including fake NFTs or replicas of rare in-game items being sold as authentic.

- **Example**: In virtual environments like **Roblox** or **Minecraft**, some users may attempt to sell counterfeit versions of popular virtual items, such as rare skins or avatars. This creates a risk for buyers

143

who believe they are purchasing valuable items, only to find that they are either fake or do not exist.

3. **Dispute Resolution in the Metaverse**: **Dispute resolution** in virtual spaces presents unique challenges, as the parties involved may be located in different countries, and the platform itself may be governed by laws that differ from those of its users. Traditional legal mechanisms may not be well-equipped to handle disputes in digital environments, so alternative methods such as **arbitration, mediation**, and **platform-based dispute resolution** are increasingly used.

   o **Example**: Some metaverse platforms, like **Decentraland**, provide built-in mechanisms for resolving disputes between users or between users and the platform itself. For example, if a buyer believes that a virtual land sale was fraudulent or that an NFT was misrepresented, they can file a complaint with the platform's **support team**, which may offer a mediation process to resolve the issue.

   o **Arbitration Clauses**: Many platforms now include **arbitration clauses** in their terms of service, which require users to resolve disputes through arbitration rather than through traditional litigation. These clauses often mandate that users agree to resolve any issues with the platform through **private arbitration** rather than through the court system.

- **Example**: In platforms like **Fortnite**, if a user has an issue with a virtual purchase or an in-game ban, the terms of service may specify that any disputes must be handled through arbitration, meaning the user cannot file a lawsuit in a traditional court but must instead rely on a neutral third party to resolve the matter.

Conclusion

Contract law and transactions in the metaverse are rapidly evolving to accommodate the growing complexity of virtual economies and digital assets. Legal frameworks must adapt to ensure that users are protected when buying, selling, or trading virtual goods and services. **Consumer protection, fraud prevention**, and **dispute resolution** are essential components in maintaining a fair and transparent metaverse where all users can confidently engage in transactions.

As the metaverse continues to expand, it will be crucial for both platform operators and users to understand their legal rights and responsibilities. With the rise of virtual goods, NFTs, and cryptocurrency, platforms must establish clear and enforceable terms of service, implement strong fraud protection measures, and provide efficient dispute resolution processes to ensure a safe and trustworthy environment for all participants.

CHAPTER 16

THE ETHICS OF VIRTUAL REAL ESTATE: OWNERSHIP VS. EXPLOITATION

The Ethics of Owning, Selling, and Speculating in Virtual Spaces

The concept of **virtual real estate** has become a central feature of the metaverse, with platforms like **Decentraland**, **The Sandbox**, and **Cryptovoxels** offering users the opportunity to purchase, develop, and sell virtual land. However, as with physical real estate, the buying, selling, and speculation of virtual spaces raise important **ethical questions** about ownership, exploitation, and the impact on virtual communities. While virtual real estate can offer opportunities for creativity, investment, and social interaction, it also has the potential to create **inequities** and **speculative bubbles** that may harm the long-term sustainability and inclusivity of virtual spaces.

1. **Ownership of Virtual Real Estate**: Virtual land in the metaverse is typically bought and sold through **blockchain technology**, which provides a **transparent** and **immutable record** of ownership.

Ownership of virtual real estate gives the buyer exclusive rights to use, develop, and sell the land. However, the question of who **owns** the metaverse and how ownership is distributed raises **ethical concerns** about fairness and access.

- **Example**: In **Decentraland**, users can purchase virtual land as NFTs, which grants them exclusive ownership rights to a particular parcel of land. This ownership allows them to create virtual buildings, art galleries, or social spaces. However, these digital properties can be costly, and only individuals or companies with significant financial resources may have the ability to acquire desirable plots of land, leading to concerns about **accessibility** and **economic inequality**.

- **Ethical Concerns**: One key issue is whether virtual land should be **owned** by private individuals or corporations at all. Given that the metaverse is still in its early stages, there are concerns about the monopolization of virtual space by wealthy investors who could control large portions of the metaverse, limiting access for creators, small businesses, and everyday users. This type of control could stifle creativity and hinder the growth of diverse and inclusive virtual communities.

2. **Selling Virtual Real Estate**: The act of **selling** virtual real estate has become a popular way for investors to profit from the appreciation of virtual land prices. However, the ethical implications of this practice depend on the transparency, fairness, and impact of these transactions on the wider virtual economy and community.

   o **Example**: **The Sandbox** allows users to buy and sell virtual land using **SAND** tokens. Some early investors in virtual land have made significant profits by purchasing undervalued land and selling it later at a higher price. These transactions can benefit the individual seller, but they may also contribute to an **artificial inflation** of land prices, making it more difficult for new users to access land or participate in the virtual economy.

   o **Ethical Concerns: Speculative selling** of virtual real estate can lead to **artificial price inflation**, where land is bought and sold not for the purpose of development or community building but as a **commodity** for investment. This speculative behavior can drive up land prices, pricing out individuals or small businesses who may want to use the land for creative or community-building purposes.

3. **Speculating in Virtual Real Estate**: **Speculation** in virtual real estate has been likened to real-world **housing market speculation**, where investors buy land with the expectation that it will increase in value over time. While this practice can lead to profitable returns for speculators, it also raises important questions about the **social responsibility** of investors and the potential **negative consequences** for the virtual environment.

- o **Example**: In **Decentraland**, virtual land has been sold for millions of dollars, with some investors purchasing large parcels of land with the hope that the value will increase as more users and brands enter the platform. However, if the land is not developed and remains vacant, it can lead to **underutilized virtual spaces** and an **artificial scarcity** of available land.

- o **Ethical Concerns**: Speculation can lead to the **commodification** of virtual space in a way that prioritizes profit over creativity, community building, and accessibility. If large corporations or wealthy individuals control most of the virtual land in a metaverse platform, it could create an environment where only those with significant financial resources can afford to participate in or benefit from virtual spaces. This raises questions about whether the metaverse should be a space for **collaboration and innovation** or simply a marketplace for investment.

Impact of Virtual Real Estate on Virtual Communities

The practice of owning, selling, and speculating on virtual real estate has profound implications for the **communities** that inhabit these virtual worlds. While virtual real estate can facilitate the creation of vibrant, dynamic communities, it can also **disrupt** or **fragment** communities if not handled ethically. The availability and distribution of virtual land play a major role in determining the **diversity**, **accessibility**, and **social dynamics** of virtual spaces.

1. **Impact on Community Development**: The ownership of virtual real estate directly influences the development of virtual communities. When land is owned by a few wealthy individuals or corporations, it can create an unequal distribution of resources, leading to **social stratification** and **exclusive spaces** that may alienate certain groups of users.
   - o **Example**: In **Second Life**, virtual communities have flourished around user-created spaces such as clubs, shops, and social hubs. However, the

ownership of these spaces is often concentrated in the hands of a few, which can lead to monopolies on certain areas of the virtual world, effectively excluding smaller creators or users from participating in these popular spaces.

o **Ethical Concerns**: When virtual real estate is used exclusively for **profit-driven motives**, it can hinder the development of creative and diverse communities. If only those who can afford to buy land have the opportunity to create social spaces, it may lead to a lack of inclusivity and stifle grassroots community development. This concentration of land ownership can contribute to the **exclusion** of marginalized groups or smaller creators who do not have the financial means to compete.

2. **Gentrification in Virtual Worlds**: **Virtual gentrification** is an emerging concern as virtual real estate becomes more valuable. Just as real-world gentrification leads to the displacement of lower-income communities, virtual gentrification could push out smaller users or independent creators who cannot afford to keep up with rising land prices. This process can result in **homogenized spaces** that prioritize commercial interests over creativity, culture, and community-building.

- o **Example**: In **The Sandbox**, large corporations like **Atari** and **Snoop Dogg** have invested heavily in virtual land, developing branded spaces for commercial use. While this can bring visibility and investment to the platform, it may also drive up land prices, making it more difficult for individual creators or smaller brands to enter the space.

- o **Ethical Concerns**: The commercialization of virtual spaces, driven by large-scale land investments, can create virtual environments that are less about **user experience** and more about **profit generation**. This could lead to the creation of exclusive, branded areas that feel more like shopping malls than immersive, creative spaces. The growing divide between commercial enterprises and independent creators can contribute to the erosion of virtual spaces as **community-driven environments**.

3. **Environmental Impact of Virtual Land Development**: Just as physical real estate development can lead to environmental degradation in the real world, virtual land development in the metaverse can have **ecological consequences** in terms of **server usage** and **energy consumption**. The **energy footprint** of virtual spaces, particularly those relying on blockchain and

cryptocurrency-based transactions, has been a topic of growing concern.

- o **Example**: Platforms like **Decentraland** and **The Sandbox** use blockchain technology to verify land ownership and transactions, which can result in high energy consumption due to the computational power needed to process these transactions. The environmental impact of maintaining these decentralized systems can undermine efforts to create sustainable, environmentally-conscious virtual communities.

- o **Ethical Concerns**: The environmental impact of virtual real estate development is an ethical issue that needs to be addressed as the metaverse expands. Just as we are increasingly aware of the environmental consequences of physical real estate development, it is important to consider the **carbon footprint** of digital land creation and ownership. Sustainable development practices should be implemented to ensure that virtual spaces do not contribute to **resource depletion** or **environmental harm**.

Conclusion

The ethics of virtual real estate ownership, selling, and speculation in the metaverse are complex and multifaceted. While virtual land offers new opportunities for creative expression, economic growth, and community building, it also raises significant ethical challenges related to **accessibility**, **inequality**, and the **impact on virtual communities**. As the metaverse continues to develop, it is crucial to balance the interests of investors and creators with the need to foster **inclusive**, **diverse**, and **sustainable** virtual environments.

Virtual real estate should be seen not just as a commodity to be bought and sold, but as a **shared resource** that has the potential to shape the future of digital spaces. Ethical considerations must guide decisions about land ownership, development, and speculation to ensure that the metaverse remains a space for creativity, collaboration, and community-building, rather than one dominated by economic exploitation and monopolization. By fostering a more **equitable** and **transparent** virtual economy, we can create virtual worlds that are welcoming to all users, regardless of their financial resources.

CHAPTER 17

FREE SPEECH VS. REGULATION: CENSORSHIP AND MODERATION IN VIRTUAL WORLDS

The Balance Between Free Speech and Protecting Users from Harm

One of the most pressing ethical dilemmas in the metaverse is how to balance **free speech** with the need to **protect users** from harmful content. As virtual spaces become increasingly popular, they are evolving into platforms for social interaction, business, entertainment, and more. This rapid growth brings forth a complex challenge: **how to foster open dialogue** while ensuring that users are **protected from harmful, offensive, or illegal content**.

1. **Free Speech in the Metaverse**: **Freedom of speech** is a fundamental human right that allows individuals to express their thoughts, opinions, and ideas without fear of censorship or retribution. In virtual environments, users expect the same freedoms they enjoy in physical spaces or on traditional online platforms. Virtual worlds often provide open forums for self-

156

expression, creativity, and discussion, with the potential for users to form communities, voice opinions, and engage in debates.

- o **Example**: In platforms like **VRChat**, users can express themselves in real-time through their avatars, voice communication, and text chat. This ability to communicate freely is integral to the social experience in the metaverse, where users engage in discussions ranging from casual conversation to more in-depth debates.

- o **Ethical Concerns**: While **free speech** is a valued principle, it can be problematic in virtual spaces where speech may cross the line into harmful or abusive behavior. The challenge is determining where to draw the line between **acceptable speech** and **harmful content** (such as **hate speech**, **harassment**, or **misinformation**) while still respecting users' freedom to express themselves.

2. **Protecting Users from Harm**: In contrast to the principle of free speech, the need to protect users from **harmful content** is just as important. The metaverse, like other online platforms, can be a breeding ground for **toxic behaviors**, including **harassment**, **bullying**, and **hate speech**. Users may encounter offensive content, cyberbullying, explicit

materials, or even illegal activities that can damage their emotional well-being or infringe upon their rights.

- o **Example**: In **Horizon Worlds**, Meta's virtual space, reports of **sexual harassment** and **abusive behavior** from users led to increased calls for stronger moderation policies. Meta has since implemented several safeguards, such as an **"personal boundary"** feature to prevent inappropriate interactions and improve user safety.

- o **Ethical Concerns**: The dilemma arises when virtual platforms try to regulate harmful speech and content without overstepping into censorship. The challenge is ensuring that **moderation policies** are fair and transparent, protecting users from harm while also respecting individual freedoms.

Case Studies: Banning, Content Filtering, and Self-Regulation

To address the delicate balance between free speech and protecting users, many virtual worlds have adopted various methods of **content regulation**. These methods include **banning**, **content filtering**, and **self-regulation**, all of which aim to prevent harm while fostering a positive user experience. Let's explore how different virtual platforms handle these issues, with a focus on **case studies** in the metaverse.

1. **Banning Users and Content**: One of the most common ways to address harmful behavior in virtual worlds is by **banning** users or content that violates platform rules. Bans can range from **temporary suspensions** to **permanent removal** from the platform. While banning is an effective way to remove harmful users, it raises ethical concerns about **freedom of expression** and **the right to appeal**.

   o **Example**: **Roblox** has faced challenges with **toxic behavior**, such as bullying, hate speech, and inappropriate content, especially considering the platform's large underage user base. To combat this, Roblox employs a **moderation system** that flags inappropriate content in chat and virtual interactions, with users who violate guidelines often receiving temporary or permanent bans. However, some users have argued that Roblox's moderation policies are inconsistent and that the appeal process for banned users is not always transparent.

   o **Ethical Concerns**: The ethical issue with banning is the potential for **overreach** or **inconsistent enforcement**. Users may feel that their right to free speech is violated when they are banned for behaviors that they believe are within their rights. Furthermore, there are concerns about **false positives** in automated content moderation systems, which may unjustly penalize users for harmless content or expressions.

2. **Content   Filtering**: **Content filtering** is another tool used to regulate harmful speech and actions in virtual worlds. Filtering involves automatically scanning user-generated content, including chat messages, images, and avatars, and blocking anything deemed inappropriate or offensive. This approach is often used in conjunction with human moderators to provide more comprehensive oversight.

    o   **Example**: **Fortnite** uses an automatic content filtering system to scan text chat messages for inappropriate language or content. This filtering system prevents offensive or harmful words from being typed in chat, thus reducing the risk of bullying or harassment. Additionally, Fortnite employs **community reporting** mechanisms, allowing players to report toxic behavior that the system may not have caught.

    o   **Ethical Concerns**: Content filtering can be highly effective in blocking harmful language, but it also presents challenges. Automated systems may be **overly broad**, leading to the

censorship of content that is not harmful (such as political discussion or personal opinions). Additionally, content filtering systems are not perfect and may fail to detect subtle forms of harm, such as **microaggressions** or **indirect harassment**.

3. **Self-Regulation and Community Moderation**: Some virtual platforms empower users and communities to regulate their own behavior, allowing them to set standards for acceptable conduct. **Self-regulation** and **community moderation** involve giving users the tools to report harmful content, flag inappropriate behavior, and create their own rules for interaction within virtual spaces.

   o **Example**: VRChat offers a unique approach to moderation by allowing **community-led reporting** and **self-regulated behavior**. Users can block or mute other players, and moderators are often members of the community rather than platform employees. This creates a decentralized approach to moderation, where the community has a direct say in maintaining order.

   o **Ethical Concerns**: While self-regulation can foster a sense of community responsibility and empowerment, it also comes with challenges. It can lead to **unequal enforcement** of rules, where some communities may be more tolerant of harmful behaviors, while others may be overly strict. Additionally, self-regulation may result in **vigilantism**, where users take matters into their own hands and engage in **harassment** or **exclusion** against individuals they deem undesirable.

Conclusion

The tension between **free speech** and **protecting users from harm** is one of the most significant ethical challenges in virtual worlds. As the metaverse continues to evolve, platforms must find ways to balance these competing interests. **Banning users, content filtering**, and **self-regulation** are some of the primary methods employed to maintain a safe and inclusive environment while respecting individuals' right to free expression.

However, these methods raise important ethical questions about the **limits of moderation**, the **consistency** of enforcement, and the **impact on community dynamics**. As virtual spaces grow and diversify, it will be essential to develop moderation systems that are transparent, fair, and adaptable to the unique challenges of virtual environments. By fostering **open dialogue, ethical guidelines**, and **community-driven moderation**, the metaverse can become a space where users can engage in meaningful interaction without compromising safety or freedom of expression.

CHAPTER 18

CORPORATE POWER IN THE METAVERSE: WHO CONTROLS THE VIRTUAL WORLD?

The Influence of Big Tech Companies and Platform Owners in Shaping the Metaverse

The **metaverse**, a rapidly growing virtual environment where users can interact, socialize, and transact, is being largely shaped by **big tech companies** and **platform owners**. These corporate giants wield significant influence in the design, governance, and economics of the metaverse, and their decisions have far-reaching consequences for users and creators. The way these companies approach issues such as platform development, data collection, user behavior, and monetization impacts the overall experience of the metaverse and raises ethical concerns about **power** and **control**.

1. **Big Tech Companies and Their Role**: Large technology companies such as **Meta (formerly Facebook)**, **Microsoft**, **Google**, and **Tencent** are at the forefront of building the metaverse. These corporations

164

are investing heavily in virtual reality (VR), augmented reality (AR), blockchain, and artificial intelligence (AI) to create immersive digital environments. As the owners and operators of platforms like **Horizon Worlds**, **Minecraft**, and **Roblox**, these companies have the ability to define the rules of engagement and set the direction of the metaverse's development.

- o **Example**: **Meta**, under the leadership of Mark Zuckerberg, has aggressively positioned itself as the leader in the development of the metaverse with its vision of creating an interconnected virtual space for work, play, and socializing. Meta's **Horizon Worlds** allows users to interact, create, and participate in virtual experiences. However, Meta's control over this platform means it can enforce rules and policies that directly affect users' experiences, from content moderation to privacy protocols.

- o **Example**: **Microsoft** has also entered the metaverse through its **Microsoft Mesh** platform, which integrates **AR/VR** capabilities with existing business applications. By leveraging tools like **HoloLens** and cloud computing, Microsoft is positioning itself as a leader in virtual business environments, particularly for collaboration and productivity in virtual spaces.

Its influence allows it to dictate the ways in which businesses, organizations, and individuals interact within its virtual environments.

2. **Platform Owners as Gatekeepers**: The owners of metaverse platforms have significant control over the experience of their users, as they create and enforce the terms under which users can interact, create, and transact in virtual worlds. Platform owners establish the **rules of engagement**, dictate what content is allowed, and determine how economic systems operate within these environments. They also often control access to virtual goods, services, and experiences, shaping users' behavior through mechanisms like **monetization**, **advertising**, and **virtual currencies**.

   o **Example**: In **Roblox**, a platform that allows users to create games and virtual experiences, the platform owner, **Roblox Corporation**, governs the rules of game creation, content moderation, and transactions. Roblox's proprietary **Robux** currency is central to the economy of the platform, and platform fees, including those for developers, are a major revenue source for the company. By controlling the flow of virtual currency and content creation, Roblox Corporation maintains a dominant position in shaping the experience for creators and players alike.

o **Example**: Similarly, **Fortnite**, owned by **Epic Games**, has developed a metaverse-like platform where players can socialize, attend concerts, and engage in a variety of activities. The integration of brand collaborations, in-game purchases, and the control over access to exclusive content demonstrates the power that platform owners have in dictating how users interact within these virtual environments.

3. **The Role of Big Tech in Standardizing the Metaverse**: As big tech companies push to develop their own versions of the metaverse, there is a significant concern about the **standardization** of these virtual spaces. Each platform has its own vision, set of rules, economic model, and technological requirements. As a result, the metaverse remains fragmented, with different systems, currencies, and experiences that do not necessarily interoperate. **Corporate influence** can lead to a lack of compatibility and user control, as the platforms may prioritize their own interests over an open, decentralized, and interoperable metaverse.

o **Example**: The **interoperability** between different virtual worlds remains a major challenge. For example, items and avatars

167

purchased in one virtual world (e.g., **Decentraland**) cannot be easily transferred to another (e.g., **Roblox**), as these platforms operate independently with their own systems and rules. This creates a fragmented experience for users who may wish to use the same assets across multiple environments.

The Dangers of Monopolies and Overreach in Virtual Spaces

The concentration of power and control in the hands of a few large corporations can have serious consequences for the future of the metaverse. **Monopolies** and **corporate overreach** in virtual spaces can stifle innovation, limit user choice, and create an unlevel playing field, especially for smaller creators, developers, and businesses. Here are some of the potential dangers of monopolistic behavior in virtual worlds:

1. **Monopolies and Limited Competition**: When a few large tech companies dominate the metaverse space, they can **monopolize the market**, preventing smaller competitors from entering or thriving. These monopolistic practices could result in reduced **competition**, higher prices for virtual goods and services, and limited innovation. In a monopolistic environment, users may face fewer choices and be forced to interact

168

with the same platforms over and over again, limiting the diversity and richness of the virtual experiences available.

- o **Example**: Meta's dominance in the virtual reality space with its Oculus products and Horizon Worlds raises concerns about market concentration. If Meta becomes the dominant platform in the metaverse, smaller competitors may struggle to gain traction, and users could be locked into a single platform with little room for alternative services or experiences. This could discourage new ideas and technological advancements, as Meta or other big players would have the power to set the agenda.

- o **Ethical Concerns**: Monopolies can lead to an **unbalanced** distribution of power, where platform owners can dictate terms that favor their own interests over those of users or smaller creators. For example, when platform fees or restrictions become oppressive, smaller developers may not be able to thrive, limiting the creativity and diversity of virtual worlds.

2. **Corporate Overreach and User Exploitation**: The danger of corporate overreach in the metaverse also lies in the potential for **exploitation** of users. Large tech companies have access to vast amounts of personal data and can exploit this information for commercial gain. In

addition, these companies can use their power to influence user behavior, often through subtle mechanisms like **nudging** or **gamification**. These methods encourage users to spend more time on the platform, buy virtual goods, or share more personal information, sometimes at the expense of user well-being.

- o **Example**: In virtual worlds like **Fortnite** or **Roblox**, players are encouraged to purchase virtual items (skins, avatars, etc.) through in-game purchases. These purchases often rely on **microtransactions**, which can accumulate to significant amounts of real-world money. Some users, especially younger ones, may fall prey to these systems, leading to excessive spending or financial exploitation.

- o **Ethical Concerns**: Companies with monopolistic power can use their influence to push **exploitative** practices, such as aggressive advertising or manipulative user interface designs. For example, **loot boxes** or **pay-to-win** mechanics are increasingly common in games and virtual environments. These methods can disproportionately affect vulnerable users, such as minors, who may not fully understand the financial implications of their actions.

3. **Control Over Content and Censorship**: When a few large corporations control the virtual spaces where users interact, they have the ability to **censor** content or **suppress speech** that does not align with their interests or business goals. This type of corporate censorship can limit freedom of expression and negatively impact the diversity of voices within virtual worlds.

   o **Example**: In platforms like **Roblox** or **Minecraft**, certain content may be censored or removed based on the platform's policies, which are often set by the owners of the platform. While some moderation is necessary to prevent harmful or illegal content, there is a risk that corporate interests could influence what is allowed in virtual worlds, leading to the **silencing of dissenting voices** or the **marginalization** of certain communities.

   o **Ethical Concerns**: **Censorship** and content moderation can be problematic if it is driven by corporate agendas or profit motives. In the absence of a **transparent, accountable** process for moderating content, users may be excluded from virtual spaces for expressing ideas that challenge the status quo, leading to a **monolithic**, non-inclusive virtual environment.

Conclusion

Corporate power in the metaverse raises significant ethical concerns about the concentration of control and the potential for **monopolies, exploitation,** and **corporate overreach**. The influence of big tech companies in shaping the metaverse gives them the power to define user experiences, control content, and direct the flow of digital economies. While these platforms offer innovative opportunities, they also introduce serious risks related to fairness, access, and freedom of expression.

To ensure that the metaverse remains an open, inclusive, and creative space, it is crucial to address these concerns by promoting **competition**, ensuring **user protection**, and fostering **diversity** in virtual spaces. Platforms should prioritize **ethical design, transparency,** and **accountability**, and the broader virtual ecosystem must continue to evolve in a way that encourages innovation without stifling smaller creators or excluding marginalized voices. By recognizing the dangers of monopolistic control and corporate exploitation, we can work toward creating a metaverse that is more democratic, equitable, and accessible for all users.

CHAPTER 19

ETHICAL GAMING: DESIGNING GAMES WITH RESPONSIBILITY

Game Developers' Responsibility in Creating Ethical, Inclusive, and Non-Exploitative Games

As the gaming industry continues to expand and evolve, game developers bear a significant responsibility in ensuring that the games they create are not only entertaining but also ethical, inclusive, and non-exploitative. **Ethical game design** involves creating environments that promote **positive behaviors**, respect **diversity**, and avoid exploiting players for financial gain. Developers must balance their creative visions with the duty to safeguard players' well-being and foster a healthy gaming community.

1. **Inclusive** **Game** **Design**:
    An essential component of ethical game design is **inclusivity**. Games should be accessible to a wide range of players, regardless of their background, identity, or abilities. This includes incorporating diverse characters, storylines, and settings that reflect the real-world diversity of players. Games should also offer accessibility features

173

for players with disabilities, allowing them to engage with content fully.

- o **Example: The Last of Us Part II** is a widely praised game for its **inclusive storytelling**. The game features characters from diverse backgrounds, including women, LGBTQ+ individuals, and people of color. By incorporating these diverse characters in leading roles, the game challenges traditional gender and racial stereotypes and creates a more inclusive narrative experience.

- o **Ethical Considerations**: **Representation** matters not only for fostering inclusivity but also for avoiding harmful stereotypes. Game developers must ensure that characters are portrayed with respect, complexity, and dignity. Games that perpetuate harmful stereotypes or exclude marginalized groups may contribute to negative social attitudes or feelings of alienation among players.

2. **Avoiding Exploitative Practices**: Developers must also be cautious of creating games that exploit their players, particularly in regard to **time commitment, mental health**, and **monetary spending**. This includes being mindful of game mechanics that

encourage excessive playtime, stress players out, or exploit players' emotional vulnerabilities.

- o **Example**: Games like **Fortnite** and **Candy Crush** use **reward systems** and constant challenges to keep players engaged and returning. While this can increase enjoyment, it can also lead to addictive behaviors, especially among younger players. **Social validation** through rankings, achievements, and leaderboards can also drive unhealthy competition, pushing players to spend more time and money on the game than they initially intended.

- o **Ethical Considerations**: Developers should design games that prioritize **player well-being** and offer healthy gameplay experiences. This could mean avoiding mechanics that encourage **compulsive play** (e.g., daily login bonuses or limited-time events) or that exploit emotional triggers to increase spending.

3. **Promoting Positive Social Interaction**: Another ethical responsibility of game developers is ensuring that their games foster **positive social interactions** and discourage **toxicity**. Online multiplayer games often expose players to toxic behaviors such as **harassment, bullying,** and **hate speech**. Developers must create and enforce systems that encourage respectful

communication and provide tools to report and address inappropriate conduct.

- o **Example: Overwatch** and **League of Legends** have implemented systems like **player-reporting** and **behavioral penalties** to address toxic behavior. These systems are designed to maintain a positive and respectful environment for all players, though there is always room for improvement in ensuring that penalties are consistent and effective.

- o **Ethical Considerations**: Developers should not only create reporting tools but also encourage positive behaviors through incentives, such as **honor systems** that reward players for being cooperative and respectful. Developers must also take action to protect vulnerable players, including **minors**, from inappropriate content or behavior.

The Role of In-Game Purchases, Loot Boxes, and Microtransactions

In recent years, in-game purchases, **loot boxes**, and **microtransactions** have become a prominent feature of the gaming industry. While these monetization strategies can provide developers with a steady revenue stream, they also raise ethical

The Ethics of Virtual Worlds

questions, especially when it comes to **exploitation, transparency**, and **player trust**.

1. **In-Game Purchases and Microtransactions**: **In-game purchases** allow players to buy virtual goods, such as skins, costumes, or other cosmetic items. **Microtransactions** are a form of in-game purchase that typically involves small payments for digital items or benefits. These transactions are usually designed to enhance the player's experience, but they can also be used as a way to extract more money from players, often in subtle or coercive ways.

   o **Example**: **Fortnite** and **Apex Legends** are popular free-to-play games that rely heavily on **cosmetic microtransactions**. Players can buy skins, emotes, and battle passes, but these items do not provide any gameplay advantages. While the system is largely based on **cosmetic enhancements**, these purchases can accumulate, sometimes leading players to spend significant amounts of money.

   o **Ethical Concerns**: The ethical issue with microtransactions arises when they are used to exploit players, especially when **children** or **vulnerable individuals** are involved. Some games push players toward spending money by offering **limited-time offers** or making certain

177

items available only through purchase. This can encourage players to spend money beyond their intended budget, leading to feelings of regret or financial distress.

2. **Loot** **Boxes**: **Loot boxes** are virtual items that players can purchase or earn in-game, which contain random rewards. These rewards can range from cosmetic items to powerful in-game advantages. Loot boxes often rely on the mechanics of **gambling**, as players spend money or in-game currency without knowing what they will receive.

- o **Example**: Games like **FIFA, Overwatch**, and **Star Wars Battlefront II** have included loot boxes, where players can pay real or in-game currency to open a box that contains randomized rewards. While some games limit the potential impact of loot boxes by offering purely cosmetic items, others may give players a competitive advantage based on the contents of the loot box.

- o **Ethical Concerns**: Loot boxes have drawn significant criticism for being **exploitative** and **gambling-like**, especially when they offer players a chance to obtain valuable items that impact gameplay. In some cases, loot boxes may encourage players to spend large sums of money in the hope of acquiring rare or powerful items, leading to potential **addiction** or **financial harm**. Moreover, the **lack of transparency** in loot box mechanics—such as the odds of obtaining specific items—raises concerns about **fairness** and **deception**.

- o **Example**: The controversy surrounding **Star Wars Battlefront II** illustrates the dangers of loot boxes in competitive games. Initially, loot boxes offered players the chance to unlock powerful upgrades for their characters, giving those who spent money a significant advantage over others. This created a **pay-to-win** situation, which led to backlash from players and regulators alike, eventually forcing **EA** (the publisher) to revise its approach.

3. **Ethical Considerations with Microtransactions and Loot Boxes**:

   Game developers must carefully consider the ethical implications of microtransactions and loot boxes. While these features can be a legitimate revenue model, they must be designed in a way that **respects the player's autonomy, ensures transparency**, and **minimizes exploitation**. The following are key ethical considerations:

   - o **Transparency**: Developers should make the odds of receiving certain items from loot boxes clear to players, allowing them to make informed decisions about whether to engage with these systems.

o **Fairness**: Microtransactions and loot boxes should not provide **pay-to-win advantages** that give paying players an unfair edge over non-paying players. If this happens, the game's integrity can be compromised.

o **Player Protection**: Developers should take steps to ensure that players, particularly minors, are not **manipulated** or **exploited** by in-game purchases. This may include implementing **parental controls** or limiting spending in games that target younger audiences.

Conclusion

The ethical challenges of game design in the metaverse are multifaceted, involving issues of **inclusivity, exploitation**, and **fairness**. Game developers have a significant responsibility to create **ethical, inclusive, and non-exploitative games** that promote positive behavior, respect diversity, and safeguard players' well-being. This includes **avoiding harmful business practices** such as manipulative microtransactions, loot boxes, and **pay-to-win mechanics** that can exploit vulnerable players.

180

Ultimately, the ethical design of games requires developers to carefully balance profitability with **social responsibility**. By prioritizing transparency, fairness, and player protection, game developers can create engaging, enjoyable experiences without sacrificing ethical standards or exploiting their audience.

CHAPTER 20

VIRTUAL GOODS AND THE ENVIRONMENTAL COST: IS THE METAVERSE SUSTAINABLE?

Energy Consumption, Digital Waste, and the Ecological Impact of Virtual Worlds

The expansion of the **metaverse** brings with it a significant **environmental cost**. As virtual worlds become more complex, with increasingly immersive experiences, the demand for **energy** to power these worlds and support their infrastructure grows. While the digital realm may seem intangible, its environmental footprint is very real. From the energy consumption of servers that host virtual spaces to the digital waste generated by unused assets and discarded data, the metaverse presents a unique challenge when it comes to sustainability.

1. **Energy Consumption in the Metaverse**: The primary driver of environmental impact in the metaverse is the **energy consumption** required to run the complex systems that power virtual worlds. Platforms like **Decentraland, Roblox, Horizon Worlds**, and others rely

182

on **data centers** and **cloud computing** to store, process, and deliver content to users in real-time. These servers are powered by electricity, and as virtual worlds grow in scale, so too does the need for more energy.

- o **Example**: The virtual world of **Minecraft**, which attracts millions of users daily, requires substantial computational power to run its servers and provide multiplayer services. The energy required to maintain these systems can be significant, especially during peak usage periods, such as special in-game events or updates. As more games and experiences are added to the metaverse, the strain on infrastructure and energy resources increases.

- o **Environmental Concerns**: The environmental impact of **energy consumption** largely depends on the source of the electricity used to power these data centers. Many servers rely on **fossil fuels**, which contribute to **carbon emissions** and **climate change**. Even with the increasing use of **renewable energy sources**, the overall energy demand from the metaverse and virtual environments remains high, raising concerns about the **sustainability** of this digital infrastructure.

2. **Digital Waste in Virtual Worlds**: The concept of **digital waste** refers to the data and virtual assets that accumulate over time, often leading to inefficiencies and environmental harm. Just as physical waste clutters our environment, **unused data**, **obsolete virtual assets**, and **old digital content** contribute to the growing environmental burden of virtual worlds. This digital waste not only takes up storage space on servers but also increases the energy required to maintain and transfer that data.

   o **Example**: Virtual platforms like **Second Life** and **Roblox** host vast amounts of user-generated content, including **avatars**, **virtual goods**, and **3D models**. Some of these items become outdated or abandoned by users over time, contributing to **digital clutter**. This unused content must still be stored on servers, consuming energy and resources.

   o **Environmental Concerns**: As more virtual goods, avatars, and assets are created, stored, and exchanged, the data associated with them grows exponentially. If this data is not properly managed or purged, it leads to **inefficiencies** and an increase in **carbon emissions**. **Data storage** and **transmission** create an environmental impact similar to that of physical waste management.

3. **The Ecological Impact of Blockchain and NFTs**: The rise of **Non-Fungible Tokens (NFTs)** and blockchain-based assets has introduced a new level of complexity to the environmental impact of the metaverse. NFTs, which are often used to buy and sell digital art, collectibles, and virtual real estate, are typically powered by blockchain technology that relies on **proof-of-work (PoW)** consensus mechanisms. This process requires significant computational power, leading to high levels of **energy consumption**.

   o **Example**: **Ethereum**, the blockchain most commonly used for NFTs, consumes enormous amounts of energy due to its reliance on PoW to validate transactions and mint new tokens. This energy consumption has raised serious concerns about the **carbon footprint** of NFT transactions, particularly when these digital assets are bought and sold at high frequencies.

   o **Environmental Concerns**: The ecological cost of NFTs and blockchain technology is particularly concerning, given the scale of the virtual economy they are helping to create. Each transaction, from minting NFTs to transferring digital assets, requires energy-intensive operations that contribute to **global warming**. As NFT popularity surges, the energy demand associated with blockchain platforms will continue to grow unless more sustainable alternatives are adopted.

Sustainable Practices for Virtual World Development

As the environmental impact of the metaverse becomes more apparent, developers and platform owners must consider **sustainable practices** to reduce the ecological footprint of virtual worlds. Creating a more sustainable metaverse involves using energy-efficient technologies, reducing digital waste, and adopting practices that prioritize **long-term environmental health**. Here are some key sustainable practices that can help mitigate the environmental cost of virtual worlds:

1. **Transitioning to Renewable Energy Sources**: One of the most effective ways to reduce the environmental impact of virtual worlds is by powering data centers with **renewable energy sources**. By using solar, wind, and other green energy sources, companies can significantly reduce their carbon footprint and make their operations more environmentally friendly.

   o **Example**: Companies like **Google** and **Microsoft** have made significant strides toward **carbon**

neutrality, with **Microsoft** pledging to be **carbon-negative** by 2030. By transitioning their data centers to renewable energy, they can reduce the impact of their cloud services and virtual infrastructure, including virtual worlds and gaming platforms.

- o **Sustainable Practices**: Virtual world developers can work with cloud service providers that prioritize renewable energy, ensuring that the infrastructure supporting virtual worlds is powered by clean energy sources. This can greatly reduce the carbon emissions associated with running virtual environments.

2. **Optimizing Data Storage and Usage**: **Efficient data management** is key to minimizing the environmental cost of digital worlds. Developers can implement practices that reduce the storage of unnecessary data, compress files, and remove outdated content. Reducing the amount of data stored on servers decreases the energy required to maintain it, leading to a more sustainable system.

- o **Example**: Platforms like **Decentraland** and **The Sandbox** can explore ways to archive or delete unused virtual assets, such as avatars, assets, or environments that are no longer in use. This

187

would free up data storage and reduce the energy needed to maintain these assets.

- o **Sustainable Practices**: Implementing regular **data purging** policies, where outdated or unused data is cleaned up periodically, can help reduce the environmental impact of digital waste. Additionally, adopting **data compression techniques** can help reduce storage space and the energy required to transmit and access information.

3. **Adopting Energy-Efficient Blockchain Technologies**: One of the most pressing environmental concerns in the metaverse is the energy consumption of blockchain technologies. **Proof-of-work (PoW)**, used by Ethereum and other blockchains, requires substantial computational power. To address this, the industry can shift toward more energy-efficient **blockchain models**, such as **proof-of-stake (PoS)**, which consumes far less energy.

- o **Example: Ethereum 2.0**, which is transitioning from PoW to PoS, promises to reduce the energy consumption of Ethereum-based platforms. By shifting to PoS, Ethereum will significantly decrease the energy required for transaction validation, making blockchain-based virtual assets more sustainable.

○ **Sustainable Practices**: Virtual world developers should explore blockchain platforms that use energy-efficient consensus mechanisms like **PoS** or consider adopting **layer-2 solutions** that optimize transaction speed and reduce the environmental impact. Using such technologies can greatly reduce the carbon footprint of virtual asset transactions, including NFTs and virtual land purchases.

4. **Implementing Circular Economy Models**: A **circular economy** in the metaverse can minimize waste and promote the reuse and recycling of virtual assets. Rather than creating an infinite cycle of consumption and disposal, virtual worlds can implement systems that encourage **asset longevity**, **reuse**, and **repair**.

○ **Example**: In virtual worlds like **Second Life**, users have the option to recycle or repurpose digital assets. By encouraging users to trade, recycle, or reuse virtual goods instead of creating new ones, developers can reduce the constant demand for new digital goods, thus cutting down on digital waste.

○ **Sustainable Practices**: Developers can promote the use of **upgradable virtual goods** that can be reused or modified over time, rather than throwing away old assets. For instance, virtual

189

clothing and skins can be made customizable so that players can update or redesign their existing items, reducing the need for frequent purchases of new virtual goods.

Conclusion

The environmental impact of the metaverse is a growing concern, particularly in terms of **energy consumption, digital waste**, and the **ecological cost** of virtual worlds. As the metaverse expands, developers and platform operators must embrace **sustainable practices** to mitigate these effects and ensure that virtual environments remain viable in the long term. By transitioning to renewable energy sources, optimizing data storage, adopting energy-efficient blockchain technologies, and implementing circular economy models, the metaverse can be made more sustainable.

However, the responsibility for sustainability extends beyond developers. Users, creators, and companies alike must recognize the environmental cost of their actions and make efforts to reduce their own carbon footprint within virtual spaces. By fostering a culture of sustainability, the metaverse can become a digital environment that not only offers endless possibilities but also respects the planet we live on.

CHAPTER 21

THE EVOLUTION OF DIGITAL IDENTITY: FROM AVATARS TO BIOMETRIC INTEGRATION

How Digital Identities Are Evolving Beyond Avatars

Digital identity has traditionally been associated with the creation of **avatars**—virtual representations of oneself within digital spaces. In many virtual worlds and online games, avatars serve as the primary means for users to interact with one another and navigate virtual environments. However, as the metaverse continues to evolve, digital identity is expanding beyond simple avatars to include more **complex** and **dynamic representations** of individuals, incorporating not just visual personas but also data, behaviors, and even biometrics. This evolution signals a major shift in how people will present themselves, interact, and engage in virtual environments in the future.

1. **Avatars as the Basis of Digital Identity**: Avatars have long been the cornerstone of digital identity in virtual spaces. These virtual characters allow users to express their personalities, interests, and preferences in a

visual format. Avatars are often customizable, giving users the ability to create representations that align with their real-world selves or reflect fantasy personas.

- o **Example**: In **Second Life**, avatars are highly customizable, allowing users to create unique virtual representations of themselves. These avatars can be designed with different clothing, facial features, and even **body types** to reflect diverse identities. Similarly, platforms like **VRChat** enable users to interact with others using avatars that range from realistic to highly imaginative.

- o **Limitations**: While avatars provide a means for self-expression, they are still **superficial representations** of users. They mainly focus on appearance, which does not fully encapsulate the richness of a person's real-world identity. Additionally, avatars can sometimes be **limited by the platform's capabilities** in terms of visual fidelity and customization options, making them less personal and more generic.

2. **Beyond the Avatar: Integrating Data and Personalization**:

As virtual worlds become more interconnected and immersive, digital identity is evolving to include more than just **visual representation**. With advancements in

AI, **machine learning**, and **big data**, platforms are starting to incorporate **behavioral data**, **preferences**, and **user interactions** to build more sophisticated and personalized digital identities.

- o **Example**: In **Horizon Worlds**, Meta's social VR platform, users are encouraged to create more personalized avatars that reflect their identities. But beyond appearance, these avatars can evolve based on users' behavior, preferences, and interactions within the virtual space. For instance, an avatar's social interactions, communication style, and in-game actions can influence how the platform tailors future experiences and content for the user.

- o **The Role of Data**: As more personal data is generated in virtual spaces, users' digital identities will be shaped by this information. Virtual worlds can track not only **how users interact** with content but also **what they purchase, how they communicate**, and even **what decisions they make** in-game. This creates a **data-driven identity** that can be leveraged to offer more tailored experiences but also raises questions about privacy and consent.

3. **The Shift Toward Persistent Digital Identities**: One of the most profound changes in the evolution of

digital identity is the shift toward **persistent** and **cross-platform identities**. Unlike isolated avatars that exist only within specific games or environments, the future of digital identity may involve **seamless continuity** across multiple virtual worlds, online platforms, and even real-world applications.

- o **Example: Epic Games**, the creators of **Fortnite**, have built a **digital ecosystem** that connects avatars and assets across games, allowing for a **persistent digital identity** that spans different virtual worlds and experiences. If a user purchases a skin or item in one game, it could potentially be used across other Epic Games platforms, creating a **unified identity** and virtual presence.

- o **Ethical Considerations**: As digital identities become more integrated and persistent, concerns around **ownership** and **control** of one's identity will become more important. Who owns the digital identity? Does the user have control over how their identity is presented across different platforms? How can users ensure their identity is not exploited or manipulated by platform owners?

The Potential for Biometric Authentication in Virtual Worlds

As digital identities evolve, **biometric authentication** is emerging as a potential tool to provide a more secure and personalized way for users to authenticate themselves within virtual worlds. Biometric technologies, which include **fingerprint recognition, facial recognition**, and **iris scanning**, are already in use in a variety of real-world applications, such as unlocking smartphones or securing financial transactions. These technologies are now being explored as a means of enhancing digital identity in the metaverse.

1. **Biometric Authentication for Security**: One of the primary benefits of using biometric authentication in virtual worlds is the added layer of **security** it provides. By using biometric data, such as **fingerprints** or **facial recognition**, platforms can ensure that users are who they say they are, reducing the risk of **identity theft, fraud**, and **account hijacking**.

   o **Example**: Virtual reality platforms, such as **VRChat** and **AltspaceVR**, could potentially integrate biometric authentication to verify users before they enter the platform. For example, a user's **face scan** could be used to unlock their account or verify identity in an immersive virtual environment.

○ **Ethical Considerations**: The use of biometric data in virtual environments raises significant privacy concerns. Storing and managing biometric data requires careful attention to data protection laws and regulations, as well as transparency regarding how this data is used and secured. Unauthorized access or **data breaches** could expose sensitive information and compromise users' safety.

2. **Personalizing the User Experience**: In addition to security, biometric authentication can help **personalize** the user experience in virtual worlds. For example, **facial recognition technology** can be used to **mirror a user's real-world facial expressions** in real-time, creating more **authentic avatars**. By using biometrics, virtual worlds can enhance the level of immersion and realism, offering users more control over how they are represented in digital spaces.

○ **Example**: Platforms like **Facebook Horizon** (Meta's social VR platform) are exploring ways to integrate **facial tracking** with VR technology, so that users' avatars can reflect their **real-world expressions** during interactions. This could make avatars appear more lifelike and provide a richer, more authentic form of communication in virtual spaces.

- o **The Role of Biometrics in Communication**: Biometrics can also be used to track **speech patterns, body language**, and **emotional responses** in virtual interactions. For example, if a user smiles or frowns in real life, their avatar could reflect those expressions, adding an extra layer of emotional nuance to conversations in virtual worlds.

3. **Risks and Challenges of Biometric Integration**: While biometric authentication holds great promise for improving security and personalization, it also introduces significant **ethical risks** and **privacy concerns**. The most pressing issues involve the **storage** and **use** of biometric data, as well as the potential for **surveillance** and **intrusion** in users' lives.

  - o **Example**: If a virtual world uses **iris scanning** or **voice recognition** to authenticate users, there is the risk that this sensitive data could be misused. Platforms could potentially track users' movements, interactions, and emotional states, leading to concerns about **privacy invasion** and the potential for **data exploitation**.

  - o **Ethical Considerations**: To address these risks, platforms must ensure that biometric data is **securely stored, encrypted**, and **accessed only with explicit user consent**. Additionally, users should have the ability to **control** how their biometric data is used and stored, and they should have the option to **opt-out** of biometric authentication if they feel uncomfortable with it.

Conclusion

The evolution of digital identity is transforming how users present themselves and interact in virtual worlds. From the traditional use of avatars to more complex, personalized representations, digital identities are becoming **increasingly dynamic** and **data-driven**. As virtual worlds become more interconnected, the persistence and continuity of these identities across different platforms will become crucial, raising new questions about **ownership**, **control**, and **representation**.

Simultaneously, **biometric authentication** offers significant potential to enhance the **security** and **personalization** of digital identities in virtual worlds. While biometric technologies can provide a more seamless and secure user experience, they also introduce important ethical and privacy challenges. As the metaverse develops, it will be essential for developers, regulators, and users to carefully consider the ethical implications of biometric data usage and ensure that digital identities are respected, secure, and protected.

As we move into a future where digital identities are more closely tied to our real-world selves, the evolution of virtual identities, alongside the integration of biometric technologies, will continue to shape the way we interact, connect, and experience the digital world.

CHAPTER 22

NFTS AND THE FUTURE OF DIGITAL OWNERSHIP

What Are NFTs and How Do They Affect Ownership of Virtual Goods?

Non-Fungible Tokens (NFTs) have taken the digital world by storm, becoming a central feature of the metaverse. Unlike cryptocurrencies such as **Bitcoin** or **Ethereum**, which are interchangeable and have the same value, **NFTs** are **unique digital assets** that represent ownership of a specific item or piece of content, often tied to **artwork**, **virtual real estate**, or **in-game assets**. NFTs are built on **blockchain technology**, which provides a transparent and secure way to verify ownership and ensure the authenticity of digital items.

1. **Understanding** NFTs:
   An **NFT** is a digital certificate of ownership for a unique asset, typically created and stored on a blockchain, such as **Ethereum**. This technology allows users to **buy, sell,** or **trade** digital goods with a verified proof of ownership. NFTs are commonly associated with **digital art**, **collectibles**, and **virtual goods**, but their use extends to

almost anything that can be digitally represented, including **virtual real estate** and **virtual items** in video games.

- o **Example**: In virtual worlds like **Decentraland** or **The Sandbox**, virtual land and assets (such as avatars, clothing, and accessories) are often bought and sold as NFTs. These virtual assets are stored on the blockchain, ensuring that ownership is tracked and verifiable. When a user purchases a virtual property or item, they gain **true ownership** of that item, which they can later sell or trade.

2. **How NFTs Affect Ownership**: NFTs redefine the concept of **ownership** in the digital realm. In traditional digital environments, users do not truly own the items they purchase or earn within a platform. For instance, in most video games, players can buy in-game items, but these items are typically tied to their account and cannot be transferred outside the game. NFTs, on the other hand, enable **true ownership** of digital assets, where the user holds a **unique, transferable token** that proves their right to the item, often including the right to sell, trade, or transfer it.

- o **Example**: A **digital art piece** sold as an NFT represents the unique ownership of that artwork, which is stored on the blockchain. While the digital image itself can be copied and shared, the **NFT** proves ownership of the original work, and only the holder of the NFT has the right to sell or transfer it.

- ○ **Ownership vs. Copyright**: It's important to note that owning an NFT does not necessarily mean owning the **copyright** to the digital asset. In most cases, NFTs grant the holder ownership of the **tokenized asset** but not the rights to reproduce or modify the underlying content. For example, owning an NFT of a digital artwork does not automatically grant the buyer the right to **use the image commercially** unless explicitly stated in the terms of sale.

Legal and Ethical Implications of NFTs in the Metaverse

The rise of NFTs has introduced a number of **legal** and **ethical challenges** in the metaverse. As the metaverse becomes a space for buying, selling, and trading virtual goods, NFTs are at the heart of this new digital economy. However, their rapid adoption also brings concerns about **intellectual property**, **fraud**, **environmental impact**, and **regulatory oversight**.

1. **Intellectual Property Issues**:
   One of the most pressing legal concerns surrounding

NFTs is how **intellectual property (IP)** laws apply to virtual goods. Since NFTs provide ownership of digital assets but not necessarily the **copyright** or **licensing rights** of the associated content, the relationship between NFT ownership and IP law is still unclear.

- o **Example:** If an artist creates a digital piece of art and sells it as an NFT, the buyer may own the NFT and have the right to resell it, but they may not automatically have the right to use the artwork for commercial purposes (such as on merchandise). The artist retains the **copyright**, unless explicitly transferred through the sale of the NFT.

- o **Legal Concerns:** Developers and artists need to clearly define the **terms of use** and **intellectual property rights** when creating and selling NFTs. Without a standardized framework, disputes could arise regarding the **transferability of rights** or the **ownership of digital content**. Platforms selling NFTs must also implement measures to prevent the sale of unauthorized or **stolen digital goods**, as this could lead to **copyright infringement**.

2. **Fraud and Scams in NFT Markets:** The NFT space has been a breeding ground for **fraudulent activity** and **scams**, as the value of digital

assets can fluctuate dramatically. In some cases, individuals or organizations have sold **fake NFTs** or misrepresented the authenticity of the underlying assets, leading to financial losses for unsuspecting buyers.

- o **Example**: Scammers may create **fake digital art** or **NFTs** and sell them to buyers who believe they are purchasing authentic items. In some cases, the scammers may use **phishing** techniques to trick users into revealing their private keys or wallet information, allowing them to steal funds.

- o **Legal Concerns**: The rise of NFT-related scams calls for **greater regulation** and consumer protection in the NFT market. Platforms that sell or auction NFTs must have robust **verification systems** to ensure the legitimacy of the items being sold. Buyers must also be educated about the risks of purchasing NFTs, particularly in a largely unregulated market.

3. **Environmental   Impact**:
The environmental impact of NFTs has become a significant ethical issue, particularly in relation to the **energy consumption** associated with blockchain transactions. Most NFTs are built on **Ethereum**, which currently uses a **proof-of-work (PoW)** consensus mechanism to validate transactions. This process requires

vast amounts of computational power, leading to high **energy consumption** and **carbon emissions**.

- o **Example**: The **minting** of an NFT on the Ethereum network requires miners to use large amounts of electricity to process transactions. As more NFTs are minted and traded, the environmental impact grows, raising concerns about the **sustainability** of the NFT market.

- o **Ethical Considerations**: As awareness of the environmental cost of NFTs grows, there is increasing pressure on the NFT market to adopt more **eco-friendly blockchain technologies**, such as **proof-of-stake (PoS)** systems, which consume far less energy. Platforms and creators should consider the environmental implications of their involvement in the NFT space and explore more sustainable alternatives.

4. **Regulatory Oversight and the Future of NFTs**: As NFTs gain mainstream attention, there is growing concern about how they will be regulated in the future. Governments and regulatory bodies will need to determine how NFTs should be treated under existing laws, such as **taxation**, **consumer protection**, and **anti-money laundering** (AML) regulations.

- o **Example**: The **U.S. Securities and Exchange Commission (SEC)** has begun exploring how

NFTs may fit into current financial regulations. If NFTs are deemed to represent **investment contracts**, they could be subject to the same regulatory frameworks as securities, requiring issuers to comply with strict disclosure and registration requirements.

- o **Legal Concerns**: The regulatory landscape for NFTs is still unclear, and there is no consistent approach across countries or regions. Governments will need to develop legal frameworks that protect consumers from fraud, ensure fair taxation, and regulate the growing NFT market without stifling innovation.

5. **Ethical Ownership and Wealth Disparity**: The rise of NFTs has led to a new **digital economy**, but this also raises concerns about **economic inequality** and **wealth disparity**. NFTs have attracted significant interest from **wealthy investors**, and the prices for certain digital assets have skyrocketed. This creates an environment where only those with significant financial resources can access the most valuable NFTs, leaving others behind.

- o **Example**: High-profile NFT sales, such as **Beeple's digital art piece** that sold for $69 million, highlight the disparity between wealthy collectors and the broader public. The trend of **NFT speculation** and **investment** further entrenches economic inequality, as the value of digital assets can be highly volatile and inaccessible to many people.

- o **Ethical Considerations**: While NFTs have created new opportunities for artists and creators to monetize their work, the speculative nature of the market can also lead to **economic exploitation**. Developers and platforms need to consider the **ethical implications** of how NFTs are marketed and sold to ensure that creators and users are not unfairly disadvantaged by price inflation or **speculative bubbles**.

Conclusion

NFTs represent a profound shift in how ownership is conceptualized in the digital age, offering users the ability to truly own virtual assets in a way that was previously not possible. While NFTs provide exciting opportunities for creators and investors, they also raise **legal**, **ethical**, and **environmental concerns**. As the NFT market continues to expand, addressing these concerns will be essential to ensure that NFTs remain a sustainable and equitable part of the metaverse.

From intellectual property challenges and fraud risks to environmental impact and wealth inequality, the rise of NFTs in the metaverse underscores the need for responsible and thoughtful regulation. By balancing **innovation** with **ethics**, the NFT market can develop in a way that promotes transparency, fairness, and sustainability, paving the way for a more inclusive and accountable digital economy.

CHAPTER 23

AI AND AUTOMATION IN VIRTUAL WORLDS: WHO OWNS. WHAT?

Ownership and Ethics of AI-Generated Content

The rapid advancements in **artificial intelligence (AI)** and **automation** have introduced a new frontier in virtual worlds, particularly in the creation of **AI-generated content**. As AI technologies become more capable of creating digital assets—such as images, music, stories, avatars, and even entire virtual environments—questions about ownership, **authorship**, and **intellectual property** have become central to the ongoing development of the metaverse. The ability of AI to generate content raises significant **ethical** and **legal concerns** regarding who owns the content and how creators and users should be compensated for the AI-generated assets they interact with or use.

1. **The Role of AI in Content Creation**: AI is increasingly being used to create **virtual goods** in digital environments, from **3D models** and **textures** to **virtual landscapes** and **avatars**. Some AI tools are

209

capable of generating high-quality assets at a fraction of the cost and time that human creators would typically require. As AI technologies like **Generative Adversarial Networks (GANs)** or **Deep Learning** evolve, they enable developers to automate tasks traditionally done by humans.

- o **Example**: Platforms like **RunwayML** and **Artbreeder** allow users to create art, animations, and 3D models using AI-powered tools. For example, users can input a basic image or prompt, and the AI will generate complex artworks or character designs based on this input.

2. **Ethical Concerns with AI-Generated Content**: As AI-generated content becomes more prevalent, the question of **authorship** and **intellectual property (IP)** rights becomes more complicated. Traditional IP laws are designed to protect **human creators**, but when an AI system generates content, there is ambiguity regarding who should hold the rights to that content. Is it the person who trained or programmed the AI? Is it the AI itself, or is the content in the public domain since no human directly created it?

- o **Example**: If an AI-generated image is sold as an **NFT** (non-fungible token), who owns the copyright to the image—the developer who created the AI tool, the person who used the tool to generate the image, or the platform hosting the transaction? Traditional IP law struggles to address these new challenges, as it was designed to recognize human creators, not machines.

- o **Ethical Implications**: The rise of AI-generated content could undermine traditional notions of **creativity** and **authorship**, leading to concerns that artists and creators may be displaced or lose control over their work. **Fair compensation** for human creators whose work is used to train AI systems is another key ethical issue. Without clear ownership guidelines, creators might not receive fair remuneration for the use of their work in training AI algorithms.

3. **AI and the Question of Content Ownership**: As virtual worlds evolve, AI plays an increasingly important role in content creation. Whether in virtual games, social platforms, or digital art galleries, AI tools generate vast amounts of assets. The key question is whether ownership of these assets should belong to the AI developers, the users who created the content, or the platforms that host and distribute the content.

- o **Example**: A game developer using AI to generate a landscape for a virtual world may not be the **author** of the landscape in the traditional sense. While the developer might have guided the process, the AI produced the actual assets. In this case, who owns the final product? And if users interact with or modify the AI-generated landscape, do they now have the rights to the modified version?

- o **Ethical Considerations**: There must be a clear and transparent framework for ownership of AI-generated content in virtual worlds. This includes not only the **initial creation** of the content but also any **subsequent modifications** made by users. Without such clarity, users, creators, and developers may face **legal disputes** over content ownership.

How Automation Impacts Jobs and Creativity in Virtual Spaces

The introduction of **automation** in virtual worlds has transformed the way content is created, tasks are performed, and experiences are designed. While automation can enhance efficiency and reduce costs, it also raises concerns about its impact on **jobs** and **creativity** within the metaverse.

1. **Automation in Virtual World Development**: As AI and automation technologies continue to evolve, many aspects of **game development, virtual world creation**, and **content production** are becoming

automated. For example, **procedural generation**—the use of algorithms to create large-scale game worlds or environments—has already been employed in games like **Minecraft** and **No Man's Sky** to generate expansive virtual worlds with minimal human input. This process can significantly speed up development and reduce costs.

- o **Example**: In **No Man's Sky**, entire planets and ecosystems are generated algorithmically, offering players near-infinite worlds to explore. This type of **automated world-building** allows developers to create vast amounts of content without requiring manual input for each individual planet, saving time and resources.

- o **Impact on Jobs**: The automation of game development and content creation may lead to fewer opportunities for human developers and artists to engage in certain aspects of the creative process. While automation increases productivity, it can also result in a **decreased need for labor** in certain fields, particularly **manual content creation**, **art direction**, and **level design**.

2. **Impact on Creativity and Originality**: While automation offers benefits in terms of efficiency, it also poses a risk to **creativity**. As AI systems are increasingly used to generate content, there is a concern

that the **human touch**—the ability to create original, imaginative, and emotional experiences—could be overshadowed by mechanized processes. The reliance on AI-generated content might limit **artistic expression** and lead to more **formulaic** or **repetitive** designs.

- ○ **Example:** In the field of **game design**, while AI can generate procedurally-created environments, these spaces might lack the **narrative depth** or **unique atmosphere** that human designers can inject into their creations. For instance, a game that relies heavily on AI-generated landscapes may miss the **personal touch** and **storytelling** that a human designer can contribute, leading to an experience that feels more artificial or disconnected from human emotion.

- ○ **Ethical Implications:** There is a potential ethical dilemma regarding the role of AI in the creative process. **Human creators** might feel displaced by AI systems that can perform many of the tasks traditionally done by artists, writers, and developers. As automation takes over more aspects of game development and content creation, the question arises: **what is the role of human creativity in the future of virtual worlds?**

3. **AI and Job Displacement in the Metaverse**: Automation has the potential to disrupt traditional career paths within the virtual world economy. While new job opportunities may emerge, there are concerns that existing roles—such as **content creators**, **designers**, and **moderators**—could be displaced by AI and automated systems. For instance, AI-powered **content moderation** could replace human moderators, reducing the demand for people to enforce community standards and regulations.

  o **Example**: Many virtual worlds and gaming platforms use AI-driven tools to moderate content and ensure that users adhere to community guidelines. These systems can automatically flag inappropriate content, such as offensive language or images, reducing the need for manual intervention. While this increases efficiency, it could also lead to job displacement in content moderation.

  o **Impact on Creativity**: With AI taking over some tasks, human developers and creators may find their roles evolving, requiring them to focus more on **conceptualizing** and **strategizing** rather than executing routine or technical tasks. While this shift could foster more **innovative** roles in the industry, it may also create a gap in **skills** and lead

215

to job insecurity for those in more traditional positions.

4. **The Future of Creative Professions in Virtual Worlds**: Despite the challenges posed by automation, there is still room for human **creativity** and **innovation** in virtual worlds. As AI continues to evolve, humans will likely collaborate with AI systems, using automation to handle repetitive tasks while focusing on higher-level design, emotional storytelling, and artistic direction. Human creators will remain essential in ensuring that virtual worlds feel **authentic**, **meaningful**, and **engaging**.

   o **Example**: In game development, AI could be used to automate the generation of **terrain**, **objects**, and **NPCs** (non-playable characters), but human designers would still be needed to shape the **narrative**, **visual style**, and **user experience**. By combining AI's efficiency with human creativity, developers can craft more **dynamic**, **immersive**, and **innovative** virtual environments.

   o **Ethical Considerations**: It is important that the industry ensures that human creators are fairly compensated for their contributions, even as automation becomes more prevalent. The rise of AI in virtual world development should not come at the expense of **human value** or **artistic integrity**. The focus should be on **collaboration** between humans and machines, where both can contribute their unique strengths to the creation of digital worlds.

Conclusion

The intersection of **AI**, **automation**, and **digital ownership** in virtual worlds presents both opportunities and challenges. While AI is reshaping content creation and the digital economy, it also raises important questions about **ownership, creativity**, and **job displacement**. The ability of AI to generate content quickly and efficiently offers exciting possibilities for virtual worlds, but it also poses significant **ethical dilemmas**, particularly in the areas of **authorship, intellectual property**, and **workforce impact**.

As AI becomes increasingly integrated into virtual worlds, developers, creators, and users must carefully consider the ethical implications of these technologies. By balancing **automation** with **human creativity**, fostering new roles for creators, and ensuring **fair compensation** and **ownership rights**, the metaverse can evolve in a way that maximizes innovation without sacrificing the integrity of human contributions.

CHAPTER 24

THE FUTURE OF PRIVACY AND SECURITY IN VIRTUAL WORLDS

Emerging Technologies in Security: Blockchain, Encryption, and Biometric Safeguards

As the metaverse and virtual worlds continue to evolve, the need for robust **privacy** and **security** solutions becomes paramount. With users engaging in increasingly immersive and interconnected digital spaces, sensitive information such as **personal data**, **financial transactions**, and **behavioral data** is constantly being generated, shared, and stored. This creates significant security risks, as malicious actors may attempt to exploit vulnerabilities within these virtual environments. To address these concerns, emerging technologies such as **blockchain**, **encryption**, and **biometric safeguards** are being utilized to enhance the security of virtual worlds and protect users' data.

1. **Blockchain Technology for Enhanced Security**: Blockchain technology has the potential to revolutionize privacy and security in virtual worlds by providing a **decentralized, immutable ledger** for transactions and

data storage. Because blockchain operates on a network of nodes rather than a central server, it offers several security advantages, including **increased transparency, resilience against hacking**, and **data integrity**.

- o **Example**: In the context of virtual worlds, **blockchain** can be used to secure digital assets, including **NFTs**, virtual land, and in-game items. By storing these assets on a blockchain, users can verify the ownership and authenticity of virtual goods, ensuring that transactions are secure and tamper-proof. Additionally, blockchain can be employed to protect **user identities** by enabling **anonymous** and **secure transactions** without revealing personal information.

- o **Security Benefits**: Blockchain's decentralized nature ensures that there is no single point of failure, reducing the risk of data breaches or hacks. It also provides **audit trails**, allowing users and platform operators to track and verify all transactions and interactions within the virtual world, further strengthening security and accountability.

- o **Challenges and Ethical Considerations**: While blockchain provides strong security, it is not immune to risks. For example, **smart contract vulnerabilities** or flaws in the code can still expose users to potential exploits. Additionally, the **energy consumption** associated with some blockchain networks (particularly those using **proof-of-work** mechanisms) has raised environmental concerns, prompting the search for more sustainable alternatives.

2. **Encryption for Data Protection**: **Encryption** plays a vital role in safeguarding sensitive information in virtual worlds. By encoding data so that it can only be accessed by authorized parties with the correct decryption key, encryption helps protect users' personal information, financial data, and communications from unauthorized access.

- ○ **Example**: In virtual worlds, **encryption** can be used to protect **user accounts, payment systems**, and **private messages**. For example, when users make purchases in a virtual marketplace or trade NFTs, encryption ensures that their **credit card information, cryptocurrency wallets**, and **personal details** are kept secure from hackers.

- ○ **Security Benefits**: Encryption helps to mitigate the risk of **data breaches**, ensuring that even if an attacker gains access to a database, the information remains unreadable without the decryption key. In addition, **end-to-end encryption** of communications ensures that private conversations between users remain confidential and cannot be intercepted by third parties.

- o **Challenges and Ethical Considerations**: While encryption provides strong protection for user data, it can also create challenges in terms of **law enforcement access** and **data management**. In some cases, encrypted data may be difficult for platforms to access, even in response to **legal requests** or **emergency situations**. Additionally, **backdoors** or vulnerabilities in encryption algorithms could undermine user security if exploited by malicious actors.

3. **Biometric Safeguards for User Authentication**: **Biometric authentication** is increasingly being used as a method of **user verification** and **access control** in virtual worlds. Biometrics, such as **fingerprint scanning, facial recognition**, and **iris scanning**, offer a high level of security by using unique physical traits to authenticate users.

- o **Example**: Platforms like **Horizon Worlds** (Meta's social VR platform) and **AltspaceVR** are exploring the integration of **facial recognition** and **gesture tracking** to provide secure and personalized user experiences. For example, a user's **facial expressions** in the real world could be mirrored by their avatar in real time, enhancing immersion and interactivity in virtual environments.

- o **Security Benefits**: Biometric safeguards offer a highly secure method of authentication, as biometric data is difficult to replicate or steal compared to traditional methods such as passwords or PINs. This reduces the risk of **identity theft** and **account takeovers**, which are common threats in digital spaces.

- o **Challenges and Ethical Considerations**: The use of biometric data raises significant **privacy concerns**. **Facial recognition** and other biometric technologies can collect sensitive information about users without their explicit consent, leading to **surveillance** and **data misuse**. Furthermore, biometric data is **irreversible**, meaning that if it is compromised, it cannot be changed like a password. Therefore, the **storage** and **management** of biometric data must be handled with the utmost care to protect users' privacy and security.

Ethical Dilemmas in Personal Data Usage and Digital Footprints

As virtual worlds grow and become more complex, they generate vast amounts of **personal data** about users. This data, which includes **behavioral patterns**, **interaction history**, and **location data**, can provide valuable insights into user preferences and habits. While this data can be used to enhance user experiences and personalize virtual environments, it also presents significant **ethical dilemmas** regarding **privacy**, **data ownership**, and **surveillance**.

1. **Privacy Concerns and Data Ownership**: One of the most pressing ethical issues in virtual worlds is the **ownership** and **control** of personal data. In many virtual platforms, users unknowingly or unintentionally give up control of their data by agreeing to **Terms of Service (ToS)** or **End User License Agreements (EULAs)**. These agreements often allow platforms to collect, analyze, and monetize user data, often without fully disclosing how the data will be used.

   o **Example**: **Facebook** (now Meta) has been criticized for its handling of **user data** on its platform, particularly in terms of **targeted advertising**. In virtual environments, similar concerns arise regarding how platforms collect and monetize **user behavior**, such as which virtual goods they purchase, which areas of the virtual world they visit, and who they interact with.

- o **Ethical Considerations**: The collection and usage of personal data without explicit consent or understanding can lead to **privacy violations** and **exploitation**. Users should have **control** over their own data and be aware of how it is being used, especially when it comes to **behavioral tracking** and **advertising**. Platforms should prioritize **user consent** and offer transparent data usage policies, allowing users to opt-in or opt-out of certain data collection practices.

2. **Surveillance and Data Exploitation**: With the growth of immersive technologies like **VR** and **AR**, there is an increasing potential for **surveillance** within virtual spaces. Platforms can collect **detailed insights** into user behavior, including their **emotional responses**, **facial expressions**, and **social interactions**. This creates concerns about the potential for platforms to track and **exploit** user data for commercial or other purposes.

- o **Example**: In **VRChat**, the platform can monitor users' behaviors, such as which avatars they interact with, how long they engage in specific activities, and which virtual locations they frequent. While this data can enhance user

224

experience through **personalized content**, it also raises questions about the extent to which platforms can **monitor** users' actions in a way that could infringe on their **privacy**.

o **Ethical Considerations**: The ability to track and analyze users' actions in virtual worlds raises concerns about **surveillance capitalism**, where data is commodified and used to influence and manipulate user behavior. Ethical guidelines must ensure that platforms do not misuse data for **unethical purposes**, such as **manipulating** users into spending more money or influencing political beliefs. Striking a balance between **personalization** and **privacy** is key to maintaining ethical standards.

3. **The Digital Footprint in Virtual Worlds**: Every action a user takes in a virtual world—whether it's posting a message, buying an item, or interacting with others—creates a **digital footprint** that can be tracked and analyzed. While this data is valuable for platform operators and advertisers, it also raises concerns about long-term **data retention** and **user autonomy**.

o **Example**: A player in **Fortnite** might spend years building a virtual identity and reputation, including purchasing virtual goods, interacting with other players, and participating in in-game events. However, this data may be retained indefinitely by the platform, creating a permanent digital record of their activities.

- ○ **Ethical Considerations**: One of the key concerns is whether users should have the **right to erase** their digital footprints or **delete** their data entirely. As the **right to be forgotten** becomes a more pressing issue in the digital age, virtual world operators must consider how they handle **user data retention**, offering users the ability to **control** and **manage** their digital footprints. Users should be able to delete their data or transfer it to another platform if they choose to leave a virtual world, ensuring that they retain control over their personal information.

Conclusion

As virtual worlds and the metaverse continue to expand, the future of **privacy** and **security** will be defined by the adoption of emerging technologies like **blockchain, encryption,** and **biometric safeguards**. These technologies offer promising solutions to the challenges of securing digital spaces and protecting users' sensitive information. However, they also raise important **ethical dilemmas** regarding **data ownership, privacy,** and **surveillance**.

The key to navigating these challenges will be to ensure that virtual world platforms prioritize **transparency, user consent, and privacy rights**. By adopting ethical practices that balance the need for **personalization** and **security** with respect for **user autonomy**, virtual worlds can evolve into spaces that protect users' rights and foster trust, while still offering the innovative and immersive experiences that the metaverse promises.

CHAPTER 25

CASE STUDIES IN VIRTUAL WORLD ETHICS: LESSONS FROM THE PAST

Examples from Second Life, Fortnite, and Other Virtual Platforms

To understand the ethical challenges of virtual worlds and the metaverse, it's helpful to examine **real-world case studies** from platforms like **Second Life**, **Fortnite**, and other virtual environments. These examples highlight the ethical issues that arise in areas such as **user behavior**, **content moderation**, **economic transactions**, and **community management**. By analyzing these cases, we can glean valuable lessons about the importance of ethical considerations in shaping virtual spaces.

1. **Second Life: A Pioneer in Virtual Worlds Ethics**
   Second Life, created by **Linden Lab** in 2003, is one of the earliest and most influential virtual worlds. It allowed users to create their own avatars, build virtual property, and interact socially in an open-ended digital space. Over the years, **Second Life** has faced numerous ethical

challenges, from issues of **intellectual property (IP)** to **user conduct**.

- o **Example**: One of the key ethical concerns in **Second Life** has been around the ownership of **user-generated content**. In the early days of the platform, there was confusion and disagreement about who owned the virtual goods and assets that users created. While **Linden Lab** claimed ownership of the platform, users could create and sell their own items. However, the platform's **Terms of Service (ToS)** had clauses that allowed Linden Lab to use these assets without clear compensation for creators, raising concerns about **exploitation** and **lack of ownership rights** for users.

- o **Lesson**: The **ownership of digital goods** and the rights of content creators are fundamental ethical issues in virtual worlds. **Clear and fair intellectual property policies** are necessary to prevent the **exploitation** of user-generated content. Developers must ensure that users have control over the assets they create, and that their contributions are properly valued and protected.

2. **Fortnite: A New Era of Virtual Economy and Ethical Dilemmas**

Fortnite, developed by **Epic Games**, has grown into one of the most popular multiplayer games, known for its **free-to-play model**, **cosmetic microtransactions**, and **virtual events**. However, Fortnite has faced its own set of ethical challenges, particularly around **monetization, in-game purchases**, and **player behavior**.

- o **Example**: One of the most controversial ethical issues in **Fortnite** has been the inclusion of **loot boxes** and other in-game purchases. Although the game itself is free to play, Epic Games has heavily monetized it through the sale of **cosmetic items**, such as skins and emotes, as well as a **battle pass** that grants additional rewards. This model has been accused of encouraging **compulsive spending** and **gambling-like behavior**, especially among younger players who may not fully understand the financial implications of in-game purchases. The **randomized nature** of loot boxes in particular has raised concerns about the **psychological impact** of encouraging players to spend money on uncertain rewards.

- o **Lesson**: The ethical dilemma of **pay-to-win mechanics** and the potential for **gambling addiction** in virtual environments must be addressed with **transparency** and **responsible monetization practices**. Developers must ensure that in-game purchases are **fair, non-exploitative**, and that they do not create an unfair advantage for players who spend more money. Furthermore, **parental controls** and **spending limits** should be put in place to prevent children from falling victim to these practices.

3. **World of Warcraft: The Ethics of Player Behavior and Gold Farming**

    World of Warcraft (WoW), one of the most popular MMORPGs, has faced numerous ethical challenges related to **player behavior**, **gold farming**, and **cheating**. One of the most significant ethical issues in WoW is the practice of **gold farming**, where players use bots or manual labor to earn in-game currency, which they then sell for real-world money.

    o **Example**: **Gold farming** in **WoW** became a widespread issue, with certain players or third-party companies creating accounts specifically to generate in-game wealth. These farmers would then sell the **gold** to other players for real money, undermining the game's **economy** and disrupting the **fairness** of the gameplay experience. This practice also raised concerns about **exploitation**, as many gold farmers were found to be working in poor conditions, often in developing countries, and were paid very little for their labor.

- ○ **Lesson**: The ethical issue of **labor exploitation** in virtual economies must be addressed by game developers. While it's important to maintain a balanced in-game economy, developers should also ensure that **players** are not **exploited** by external entities. Platforms must take a proactive stance in preventing gold farming, whether through the use of **anti-bot systems, fair trade policies**, or by limiting the sale of in-game currency to third parties.

Legal Precedents and Key Ethical Failures

As virtual worlds have grown in scale and complexity, **legal precedents** and **ethical failures** have emerged, guiding the development of future virtual platforms. Some of the most significant cases highlight the importance of **data protection, content regulation, monetary transactions**, and **platform governance**.

1. **The Case of Robux and In-Game Currency**
   Roblox, a popular online game platform, faced a major legal challenge regarding its **virtual currency, Robux**, and its practices surrounding **in-game purchases**. Roblox allowed users to buy Robux with real-world money, but many parents raised concerns about the ease with which

232

children could spend money without their consent, leading to debates about **informed consent** and **parental control**.

- o **Legal Precedent**: The **Federal Trade Commission (FTC)** in the United States has investigated platforms like **Roblox** for **misleading advertising** and the lack of clear mechanisms for users to track their spending. The ethical failure in this case stems from **inadequate parental controls** and **misleading spending models**, which allowed children to rack up large bills without fully understanding the consequences.

- o **Lesson**: Virtual worlds must provide clear, **transparent billing practices** and **spending limits** for in-game currencies. Furthermore, platform owners must ensure that there are adequate **parental controls** in place to prevent unintended purchases, especially for younger players.

2. **The Case of "Loot Boxes" and Gambling Concerns**
   One of the most significant ethical failures in virtual worlds has been the introduction of **loot boxes** and the subsequent controversy regarding their resemblance to **gambling**. **Loot boxes** are often used in free-to-play games like **Overwatch**, **FIFA**, and **Star Wars**

Battlefront II to encourage players to purchase virtual goods that contain random rewards.

- ○ **Legal Precedent**: In several countries, including Belgium and the Netherlands, loot boxes have been classified as a form of **gambling**, leading to legal action against gaming companies. In response, **EA Games** was forced to revise its loot box mechanics in **Star Wars Battlefront II**, removing the ability to gain in-game advantages through loot boxes and shifting towards purely **cosmetic items**.

- ○ **Lesson**: The legal and ethical implications of loot boxes in virtual worlds highlight the importance of **transparent practices** and **player protection**. Developers must avoid introducing elements that could lead to **gambling addiction** and **exploitative monetization practices**. Clear regulations and age-based restrictions are necessary to protect vulnerable players, especially minors.

3. **Second Life's Intellectual Property Issues**
   Second Life has faced several legal and ethical challenges surrounding **intellectual property (IP)**, particularly in terms of user-generated content and ownership rights. Users in Second Life could create and sell virtual assets, but there was ambiguity around who owned the rights to

these creations—Linden Lab (the platform owner) or the individual creators.

- o **Legal Precedent**: In one notable case, **Linden Lab** faced a lawsuit from **a user** who argued that the company had illegally used their intellectual property. This case led to significant changes in the **Terms of Service** (ToS) and clarified the rights of content creators within the virtual space.

- o **Lesson**: Virtual platforms must be **transparent** about **intellectual property rights** and clearly define who owns what content. Developers should work to ensure that creators are **properly compensated** for their work, and that ownership of virtual goods is clearly outlined in platform terms. **Fair revenue-sharing models** are essential for creating trust between users and platform operators.

Conclusion

The **case studies** presented here offer valuable insights into the ethical challenges and **legal precedents** that have shaped the development of virtual worlds and the metaverse. From **ownership of digital assets** and **content moderation** to **monetization practices** and **labor exploitation**, these examples

235

demonstrate the importance of **ethics** in creating sustainable, fair, and transparent virtual environments.

The **future of virtual worlds** depends on learning from these past mistakes and building platforms that respect **user rights**, **promote fairness**, and **ensure accountability**. By implementing **ethical practices** in areas such as **data privacy**, **content ownership**, and **monetization**, developers can create virtual spaces that are not only innovative but also responsible and inclusive for all users.

CHAPTER 26

THE ROLE OF GOVERNMENTS AND REGULATORS IN THE METAVERSE

How Governments Are Starting to Regulate the Metaverse

As the metaverse grows into an increasingly complex and integral part of digital society, governments around the world are beginning to address the need for regulation in these virtual spaces. While the metaverse promises significant opportunities for innovation, social connection, and economic growth, it also raises numerous **legal**, **ethical**, and **security concerns** that need to be addressed through appropriate governance frameworks.

1. **Early Efforts at Regulation**: Governments are beginning to look at the metaverse through the lens of existing regulatory frameworks, particularly around areas such as **data protection, intellectual property, consumer protection**, and **online safety**. In some countries, regulators are seeking to apply traditional laws and rules to virtual spaces, while others

are exploring new laws specifically designed for the unique challenges presented by virtual worlds.

- o **Example**: In the **European Union**, the **General Data Protection Regulation (GDPR)** already applies to virtual worlds and platforms. This law regulates how personal data is collected, stored, and shared, which is crucial in the metaverse where user data is integral to user experiences. For instance, **Meta (formerly Facebook)**, which is heavily involved in developing its own metaverse through **Horizon Worlds**, is subject to GDPR regulations around user privacy and consent.

- o **Example**: The **United States** has seen various **state-level** actions, such as the **California Consumer Privacy Act (CCPA)**, which governs how personal data is handled by companies operating in California. Similar to GDPR, the CCPA provides consumers with rights regarding access to, deletion of, and opting out of the sale of their personal data—critical elements in the context of virtual spaces.

2. **Financial and Economic Regulations**: As the metaverse grows, it is increasingly being viewed as an economic system in its own right, with virtual currencies, assets, and transactions. Governments are

starting to take notice of the **economic activities** happening within virtual worlds, such as buying virtual real estate, trading NFTs (Non-Fungible Tokens), and even earning income through virtual platforms. This has led to the development of **taxation** and **financial regulations** around virtual assets and transactions.

- o **Example**: In countries like **South Korea**, regulators are already discussing how to impose taxes on virtual transactions and digital assets. The South Korean government has proposed that income from **cryptocurrency trading** in virtual worlds should be taxed, as the metaverse is increasingly being viewed as a legitimate space for economic activity.

- o **Legal Considerations**: One of the most significant areas of concern is **cryptocurrency regulation**. Many metaverse platforms, such as **Decentraland** and **The Sandbox**, use cryptocurrencies (such as **MANA** and **SAND**) to facilitate purchases and transactions within the virtual space. Since cryptocurrencies are not controlled by central banks and often operate in decentralized networks, **governments are looking for ways to regulate** these digital currencies, prevent fraud, and manage their use in the metaverse's economy.

3. **Online Safety and Child Protection**: As the metaverse becomes an increasingly popular space for people of all ages, **online safety** becomes a primary concern for governments. Virtual spaces offer unique challenges for **child protection**, particularly when it comes to **cyberbullying, predators,** and **age-inappropriate content**. Governments are looking into creating laws and regulations to protect **minors** from harm while still allowing for free expression and innovation in virtual worlds.

- ○ **Example: The UK's Age Appropriate Design Code** is one example of a legislative attempt to protect children in digital spaces. The Code sets out provisions that require online services, including virtual worlds, to **prioritize children's privacy** and **protect their data**. Similar child safety regulations are emerging in other countries as well, such as the **Children's Online Privacy Protection Act (COPPA)** in the United States.

- ○ **Challenges**: Ensuring **age verification** and **content moderation** in virtual spaces is a significant regulatory challenge. Unlike traditional online platforms, virtual worlds can feature **immersive** and **interactive environments**, which can blur the lines of **age-**

appropriate content and create more difficulties for enforcement.

The Challenges of Governing a Decentralized, Global Space

One of the most significant hurdles in regulating the metaverse is that it is a **decentralized, global** space. Unlike traditional forms of governance, where specific geographical boundaries can be enforced by governments, the metaverse operates across multiple countries, cultures, and digital ecosystems. This decentralization creates significant **governance challenges** that make it difficult for any single country or regulatory body to control the space.

1. **Lack of Global Consensus:** The metaverse is not owned or governed by any single entity, and it consists of multiple platforms, virtual worlds, and services that operate independently of each other. As a result, there is no **global authority** or overarching governance structure that can enforce laws or regulations consistently across different virtual environments. Countries, and even individual states or regions, have different laws, priorities, and levels of **regulatory authority**, which can make it difficult to create a unified approach to governing the metaverse.

   o **Example: Roblox**, a popular online gaming platform, operates in numerous countries around the world, but its platform is subject to varying levels of regulation based on local laws. In the **United States**, Roblox is subject to **COPPA** (Children's Online Privacy Protection Act) when handling users under 13, while the **European Union** enforces its own **GDPR** regulations regarding data privacy. These **regional differences** create inconsistencies in how the platform is regulated and create challenges for a **global approach** to governance.

2. **Enforcing Virtual Laws in a Borderless World**: The decentralized nature of the metaverse means that it is difficult to apply traditional legal concepts, such as **jurisdiction** and **territoriality**, in virtual spaces. Virtual platforms often operate across borders, and users from different countries can interact in shared digital spaces. This makes it difficult for individual governments to enforce laws and regulations that are confined to their borders, especially when virtual worlds operate in **decentralized** or **peer-to-peer networks**.

   o **Example**: **Cryptocurrencies** and **NFTs** are commonly used in virtual worlds, but since these digital assets are **decentralized**, transactions can occur without the need for traditional banking institutions. For instance, a user in **Brazil** could purchase virtual land in **Decentraland** using

Ethereum, which is then sold to a user in **Japan**. Since these transactions are conducted through **decentralized networks** that do not adhere to any specific national jurisdiction, regulating them becomes extremely challenging.

- o **Legal Considerations**: Governments would need to either create **global treaties** or **coordinated regulations** to enforce laws related to **intellectual property** (IP), **taxation**, **privacy**, and **security** in the metaverse. This requires unprecedented levels of international cooperation and a global consensus on how to manage virtual assets and governance.

3. **Decentralized Governance Models**: In some virtual worlds, such as **Decentraland** and **Cryptovoxels**, governance is built into the platform itself through **decentralized autonomous organizations (DAOs)**. In a DAO, governance is typically managed by users who participate in **voting** or decision-making processes, which could range from content moderation to economic policies.

- o **Example**: In **Decentraland**, the **DAO** is responsible for making decisions on issues such as land sales, community guidelines, and virtual asset trading. Users who hold **MANA tokens** can vote on important platform decisions, which is a unique form of self-regulation that contrasts with traditional, centralized governance models.

- o **Challenges**: The decentralized nature of these platforms can make them **difficult to regulate** from a government perspective, especially when decisions are made collectively by the community rather than by a centralized authority. This raises questions about **accountability** and **transparency**, as well as the potential for **abuse** or **manipulation** by powerful stakeholders within the virtual community.

4. **Cultural and Ethical Diversity**: The metaverse brings together users from different cultural, legal, and social backgrounds, each with varying beliefs about **freedom of expression**, **privacy**, and **morality**. What might be considered acceptable behavior in one culture or region may not be acceptable in another. This diversity presents an ethical dilemma when trying to implement **universal laws** or **standards** for virtual spaces.

- o **Example**: The concept of **hate speech** or **harassment** in virtual worlds can vary widely depending on cultural norms. In some countries, certain forms of speech or behavior may be protected by freedom of expression laws, while in others, it may be strictly prohibited. Virtual worlds that cater to a **global audience** must navigate these differences carefully to ensure that all users feel safe and respected.

o **Ethical Considerations**: Governments and virtual platform owners will need to carefully consider how to **balance local values** with the need for **global regulation**. Ensuring that virtual worlds remain **inclusive**, **respectful**, and **free from discrimination** will require nuanced, culturally sensitive policies.

Conclusion

The regulation of the metaverse is still in its early stages, and governments around the world are struggling to keep pace with the rapid development of virtual worlds. While some countries are taking proactive steps to introduce laws around data protection, consumer rights, and taxation, the decentralized nature of the metaverse presents significant challenges. With a global audience and a complex web of virtual platforms, creating a **coordinated regulatory framework** will require international cooperation, clear legal guidelines, and ethical standards that protect users while fostering innovation.

As the metaverse continues to evolve, governments and regulators must **adapt** to the unique characteristics of this virtual environment. Balancing the interests of **innovation**, **privacy**, and **safety** will be crucial in ensuring that the metaverse remains a space where users can interact freely and securely, without infringing on the rights of others. Ultimately, the future of metaverse regulation will rely on the ability of governments, tech companies, and virtual world users to collaborate and establish frameworks that reflect the complexities of this new digital frontier.

CHAPTER 27

THE METAVERSE BEYOND THE HORIZON: A LOOK AT WHAT'S NEXT

Predictions for the Future of Digital Spaces

The metaverse, as we know it today, is just the beginning of a broader evolution of **digital spaces** that will redefine how we interact, work, socialize, and create. As technologies like **VR, AR, AI**, and **blockchain** continue to mature, the metaverse will expand and become an integral part of daily life. While it is difficult to predict every development with certainty, several trends and advancements offer a glimpse into what the **next generation of digital worlds** might look like.

1. **The Rise of Fully Immersive Virtual Realities**: In the future, virtual reality (VR) will evolve from its current state—still reliant on headsets and controllers—into **fully immersive experiences** that seamlessly blend the physical and digital worlds. With **haptic feedback**, **motion tracking**, and **sensory technology** advancing rapidly, users may soon be able to **feel, smell, and even**

taste their virtual surroundings. This evolution will create virtual spaces that feel just as real, if not more so, than the physical world.

- o **Example**: Imagine a future where you can attend a concert in a **virtual stadium** and feel the vibrations of the music, smell the crowd's excitement, or even taste the refreshments you pick up from a virtual vendor. **Full-body haptic suits** might allow users to engage physically with their avatars, providing a deeper sense of **presence**.

- o **The Impact**: These fully immersive experiences could blur the lines between reality and virtuality. This heightened sense of realism could revolutionize industries such as entertainment, education, healthcare, and remote work, allowing people to experience things they previously could only dream of—without leaving their homes.

2. **The Integration of Artificial Intelligence in Virtual Worlds**:

AI will play an even more crucial role in the metaverse's development, moving beyond just creating content and moderating interactions. Future virtual worlds will feature **AI-driven non-playable characters (NPCs)** that exhibit **deep learning** and **emotional intelligence**, making interactions with these characters feel more natural and

248

intuitive. AI could also enable **personalized virtual environments**, where users' preferences are learned and the world dynamically adapts to provide tailored experiences.

- o **Example**: In a future **metaverse** platform, AI might act as a personal assistant, helping you navigate virtual spaces, suggest activities based on your mood or interests, and even create unique content or environments for you. These AI characters might form relationships with users, offering emotional support or engaging in conversations.

- o **The Impact**: The increase in AI-driven elements will make the metaverse feel more like an **organic, living space** where the virtual world evolves based on the needs and actions of its users. However, this could raise concerns about **AI manipulation, privacy**, and **autonomy** as users interact with hyper-intelligent, emotion-driven systems that learn from their behavior.

3. **A Decentralized and User-Driven Economy**: The metaverse's future may see the rise of **decentralized economies**, where users own their assets and control their experiences. **Blockchain technology** and **smart contracts** will allow for **peer-to-peer transactions** and eliminate the need for centralized platforms, enabling

users to directly trade and sell virtual goods and services. This decentralized structure could allow for a more equitable distribution of wealth and power within virtual worlds, giving users more control over their digital identities, assets, and interactions.

- o **Example**: In the future metaverse, users could create and trade NFTs and virtual assets without intermediaries. Blockchain-based virtual currencies could facilitate transactions, and decentralized platforms might allow creators to retain ownership and profit directly from their virtual goods without sharing profits with third-party platform operators.

- o **The Impact**: A decentralized metaverse would reduce the monopoly of big tech companies, offering a more democratized version of the internet. However, it also introduces challenges around **regulation**, **security**, and **fraud prevention**—issues that would need to be addressed to ensure fair and safe economic practices.

4. **Interoperability Between Virtual Worlds**: One of the most exciting possibilities for the future of the metaverse is the idea of **interoperability** between different virtual worlds. Today, virtual environments like **Roblox**, **Fortnite**, and **Second Life** exist largely in

isolation, with few ways for users to carry over assets or identities between them. However, as the metaverse matures, the ability to **seamlessly move** between different platforms while retaining **ownership** of digital assets (e.g., avatars, NFTs, virtual land) will become crucial.

- o **Example**: In a future metaverse, you might be able to take your avatar from **Horizon Worlds** into a game on **Decentraland**, use the same clothing and accessories, and even transfer digital assets like virtual property between different worlds—creating a **unified, cross-platform experience**.

- o **The Impact**: This interconnectedness would make virtual spaces more cohesive and user-friendly, allowing users to access various platforms and experiences without the need to rebuild their identity or assets. It could open the door to a more **interconnected digital economy**, but also create challenges in terms of platform compatibility, data privacy, and the protection of intellectual property rights.

Ethical Considerations for the Next Generation of Virtual Worlds

As the metaverse continues to evolve, so too must the ethical considerations surrounding these virtual spaces. The next generation of virtual worlds will present new and unique challenges in terms of **privacy, identity, economic fairness**, and **social responsibility**. Some of the most pressing ethical concerns that need to be addressed in the future include:

1. **Privacy and Data Ownership**: In an increasingly **immersive** and **data-driven** metaverse, **privacy** will be one of the most significant ethical challenges. As virtual worlds collect vast amounts of personal data—ranging from **user interactions** to **biometric data** and **emotional responses**—it becomes critical that users retain control over their own **digital identities** and **data**.

   o **Ethical Consideration**: The future of digital privacy will require **transparency** regarding how user data is collected, stored, and shared. Users should have the right to **consent** to how their information is used and should be able to **delete or transfer** their data across different virtual platforms, ensuring that their **digital footprints** are not exploited without their knowledge.

2. **Digital Divide and Accessibility**: As virtual worlds become increasingly important for **work, social interaction**, and **entertainment**, the **digital divide**—the gap between those who have access to advanced technology and those who do not—becomes a critical issue. The next generation of virtual worlds must

ensure that these spaces are **accessible** to everyone, regardless of socioeconomic status, location, or physical ability.

- o **Ethical Consideration**: Platforms should invest in making the metaverse accessible to **underrepresented communities** and ensure that **inclusive design** is embedded in the development process. This includes offering support for individuals with disabilities and providing affordable access to the hardware and software needed to participate in these spaces.

3. **Mental Health and Well-Being**: With the increasing time spent in immersive virtual worlds, **mental health** concerns will need to be addressed. Virtual spaces can be incredibly stimulating and emotionally charged, and excessive engagement could lead to **addiction, anxiety**, or **social isolation**. Additionally, the potential for **cyberbullying, harassment**, and **toxic behavior** can negatively impact users' psychological well-being.

- o **Ethical Consideration**: Platforms should prioritize user well-being by offering resources for **mental health support, user protection**, and **content moderation**. Developers must create systems that encourage **positive interactions** and

safe environments while providing tools to combat harassment and bullying effectively.

4. **Economic Equity and Fairness**: As the metaverse becomes more economically significant, there are concerns about the **wealth inequality** that could emerge in digital spaces. Virtual real estate, NFTs, and other digital assets have already proven to be lucrative investments, but there are fears that a few wealthy individuals or organizations will monopolize these spaces, leaving others with fewer opportunities to participate in the digital economy.

   o **Ethical Consideration**: Developers and regulators must create mechanisms to ensure **economic fairness** and **equal opportunity** in virtual worlds. This could involve policies that limit speculative practices, promote equitable distribution of virtual assets, and create opportunities for **low-income individuals** to participate in the metaverse without being excluded or exploited.

5. **Ethical Governance of AI**: With the integration of AI in virtual worlds, there will be growing concerns about the ethical use of **AI-driven content** and **decision-making**. AI systems could influence how users engage with content, how they are

represented in the virtual world, and even how virtual economies function.

- o **Ethical Consideration**: It will be critical to ensure that **AI systems** are transparent, non-discriminatory, and free from biases. Developers must **account for the impact** of AI on users' **freedom of choice** and **digital autonomy**, and establish clear **ethical guidelines** for the use of AI in decision-making processes.

Conclusion

The metaverse is rapidly evolving, and while it holds immense potential to reshape how we live, work, and interact, it also presents a unique set of **ethical** and **practical challenges**. As we look to the future of digital spaces, it is essential that we develop **ethical frameworks** that prioritize **privacy, inclusivity, mental health**, and **economic fairness**. By doing so, we can ensure that the metaverse grows into a space that fosters **creativity, community**, and **equity** for all users.

The next generation of virtual worlds will be shaped by the decisions we make today about governance, regulation, and ethical standards. As the technology advances, it is critical that governments, platform developers, and users work together to create a metaverse that is not only innovative but also **responsible**, **safe**, and **inclusive** for everyone.